Campbell's

Simply Delicious Recipes

CRESCENT BOOKS
New York

NOTE: CAMPBELL'S SOUP CAN SIZES USED IN THIS BOOK

	U.S.	CANADA
1 can	10½ oz *or* 10¾ oz	284 mL (10 oz)

Editor: Angela Rahaniotis
Graphic Design and Layout: Zapp
Photography: Michel Bodson
Food Preparation: Chef Stephane Drouin
Stylist: Muriel Bodson
Accessories courtesy of Potpourri, Pier 1 Imports, Les Carreaux Ramca Ltd., La Baie.

This edition was produced by Campbell Soup Company's Publications Center, Campbell Soup Company, Campbell Place, Camden, New Jersey 08103-1799, U.S.A. and Brimar Publishing Inc., Montreal, Canada.

Campbell's SIMPLY DELICIOUS RECIPES
Managing Editor: Patricia Teberg
Contributing Editor: Alice Joy Carter
Creative Director: Stacy-Jo Mannella

Every recipe in Campbell's SIMPLY DELICIOUS RECIPES cookbook was developed and tested in the Campbell Kitchens by professional home economists.

"Campbell International" is a division of Campbell Soup Company. All of the recipes in Campbell's SIMPLY DELICIOUS RECIPES cookbook have been adapted for use by consumers in the countries where Campbell's soups are available: Canada, Australia, Mexico, the United Kingdom, Puerto Rico, the United States and New Zealand. Any questions about Campbell's soups should be directed to the Campbell Soup Company office in that country. Or write to: Campbell International, Campbell Soup Company, Campbell Place, Camden, New Jersey, 08103-1799, U.S.A.

Pictured on the front cover: Classic Family Meat Loaf (*see recipe, page 169*); Creamy Vegetable Medley (*see recipe, page 168*); Lemon-Broccoli Chicken (*see recipe, page 150*).

Microwave Cooking Times: Microwave cooking times in this book are approximate. These recipes have been tested in 650- to 700-watt microwave ovens. Foods cooked in lower-wattage ovens may require longer cooking times. Use the cooking times as guidelines and check for doneness before adding more time.

This edition published by
Crescent Books, distributed by
Random House Value Publishing, Inc.
201 East 50th Street, New York, N.Y. 10022
Random House
New York • Toronto • London • Sydney • Auckland

ISBN 0-517-08757-X
Printed in Canada

Campbell's

SIMPLY DELICIOUS RECIPES

Let cooking with Campbell's condensed soups be your recipe for success. All the great-tasting recipes in SIMPLY DELICIOUS RECIPES rely on flavorful, high-quality Campbell's soups to make cooking easy -- with delicious results!

Inside, you'll find more than 125 kitchen-tested recipes, from tempting appetizers and hearty stews to savory main dishes and tasty vegetables. The more than 250 beautiful photographs, including many step-by-step techniques, will whet your appetite and inspire you to start cooking.

Everyone at Campbell believes that great-tasting recipes begin with Campbell's Soups. From our Kitchens to yours, we hope your family and friends will enjoy these Campbell favorites!

Campbell's family of cooking soups from around the world

Campbell's® Soups bring more than 125 great-tasting recipes to you

FOOD EQUIVALENTS CHART

Bread and Cookies

1 cup (*250 mL*) soft bread crumbs	2 slices
1 cup (*250 mL*) bread cubes	2 slices
1 cup (*250 mL*) fine graham cracker crumbs	14 square crackers
1 cup (*250 mL*) fine vanilla wafer crumbs	22 wafers

Dairy

1 lb (*450 g*) margarine or butter	2 cups (*500 mL*) or 4 sticks
1 cup (*250 mL*) heavy or whipping cream	2 cups (*500 mL*) whipped
8 oz (*225 g*) cream cheese	1 cup (*250 mL*)
1 lb (*450 g*) Swiss or Cheddar cheese	4 cups (*1 L*) shredded
4 oz (*120 g*) blue cheese, crumbled	1 cup
4 oz (*120 g*) Parmesan or Romano cheese	1¼ cups (*300 mL*) grated
1 large egg	3 tbsp (*45 mL*) egg

Dried legumes

1 cup (*250 mL*) dried beans or peas	2¼ cups (*550 mL*) cooked

Fruits

1 lb (*450 g*) apples	3 medium
1 lb (*450 g*) bananas	3 medium
1 medium lemon	2 tbsp (*30 mL*) juice
1 medium orange	⅓ to ½ cup (*75 mL to 125 mL*) juice

Herbs

1 tbsp (*15 mL*) fresh	1 tsp (*5 mL*) dried

Pasta

8 oz (*225 g*) elbow macaroni, uncooked	4 cups (*1 L*) cooked
8 oz (*225 g*) spaghetti, uncooked	4 cups (*1 L*) cooked
8 oz (*225 g*) medium noodles, uncooked	3¾ cups (*925 mL*) cooked

Rice

1 cup (*250 mL*) regular long-grain rice, uncooked	3 cups (*750 mL*) cooked
1 cup (*250 mL*) quick-cooking rice, uncooked	2 cups(*500 mL*) cooked

Vegetables

1 lb (*450 g*) carrots	2½ cups (*625 mL*) sliced
1 lb (*450 g*) cabbage	4 cups (*1 L*) shredded
1 lb (*450 g*) onions (yellow)	5 to 6 medium
1 medium onion	½ cup (*125 mL*) chopped
1 lb (*450 g*) all-purpose potatoes	3 medium
1 lb (*450 g*) fresh mushrooms	3 cups (*750 mL*) sliced
1 lb (*450 g*) tomatoes	3 medium
1 lb (*450 g*) broccoli	2 cups (*500 mL*) flowerets

Miscellaneous

1 lb (*450 g*) cooked meat	3 cups (*750 mL*) diced
1 lb (*450 g*) raw boneless meat	2 cups (*500 mL*) cooked, cubed
1 lb (*450 g*) raw ground beef	2¾ cups (*675 mL*) cooked

Simply Delicious Recipes

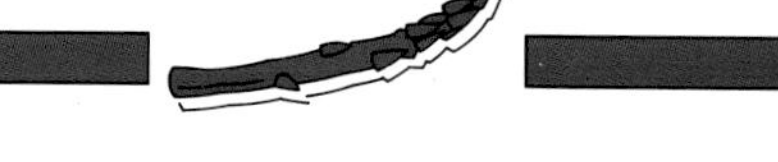

BASIL CHICKEN AND BROCCOLI POTATO TOPPER

1 can	**CAMPBELL'S condensed Cream of Broccoli *or* Cream of Chicken Soup**
1 pkg (3 oz)	**(*90 g*) cream cheese, cut up**
1 cup	**(*250 mL*) cubed cooked chicken**
1½ cups	**(*375 mL*) frozen broccoli cuts**
2 tbsp	**(*30 mL*) milk**
1 tsp	**(*5 mL*) dried basil leaves, crushed**
1 tsp	**(*5 mL*) lemon juice**
4	**hot baked potatoes, split**
	Chopped sweet red pepper for garnish

■ In 2-quart (*2 L*) saucepan over medium heat, combine soup, cream cheese, chicken, broccoli, milk, basil and lemon juice. Heat through, stirring occasionally.

■ Spoon over potatoes. Garnish with red pepper, if desired.

To microwave: In 2-quart (*2 L*) microwave-safe casserole, combine soup, cream cheese, chicken, broccoli, milk, basil and lemon juice. Cover with lid; microwave on HIGH 8 minutes, stirring halfway through heating. Continue as directed above.

Basil Chicken and Asparagus: Prepare Basil Chicken and Broccoli as above, *except* substitute 1 package (10 ounces / *285 g*) frozen asparagus spears cut into 1-inch (*2,5 cm*) pieces for the broccoli cuts.

Makes about 2½ cups (625 mL) or 4 servings.

BASIL CHICKEN AND BROCCOLI POTATO TOPPER

ARTICHOKE-CHILI DIP

1 can	**CAMPBELL'S condensed Cream of Celery *or* Cream of Chicken Soup**
2 pkgs (3 oz *each*)	**(*180 g*) cream cheese, softened**
1 can (14 oz)	**(*398 mL*) artichoke hearts, rinsed, drained and chopped**
1 can (4 oz)	**(*110 g*) chopped green chilies**
½ cup	**(*125 mL*) grated Parmesan cheese**
	Paprika

■ Preheat oven to 375 °F (*190 °C*). Meanwhile, in 1-quart (*1 L*) casserole, stir soup and cream cheese until as smooth as possible. Stir in artichokes, chilies and Parmesan.

■ Bake 15 minutes or until hot and bubbling. Stir; sprinkle with paprika. Serve with *crackers* or *tortilla chips* for dipping.

To microwave: In 1½-quart (*1,5 L*) microwave-safe casserole, stir soup and cream cheese until smooth. Stir in artichokes, chilies and Parmesan. Microwave, uncovered, on HIGH 6 minutes or until hot, stirring twice during cooking. Sprinkle with paprika. Serve as directed above.

Makes about 3½ cups (875 mL).

DILLED SALMON DIP

1 can	**CAMPBELL'S condensed Cream of Celery *or* Cream of Chicken Soup**
¼ cup	**(*50 mL*) mayonnaise *or* sour cream**
2 tbsp	**(*30 mL*) prepared horseradish**
1 tbsp	**(*15 mL*) chopped fresh dill *or* 1 tsp (*5 mL*) dried dill weed, crushed**
⅛ tsp	**(*0,5 mL*) pepper**
1 can (7½ oz)	**(*215 g*) salmon, drained and flaked**
	Fresh chopped dill *and* dill sprig for garnish

■ In medium bowl, combine soup, mayonnaise, horseradish, chopped dill and pepper. Add salmon; mix lightly. Cover; refrigerate 15 minutes.

■ To serve: Garnish dip with additional dill, if desired. Serve with *assorted cut-up vegetables* and *party rye bread* for dipping.

Makes about 2 cups (500 mL).

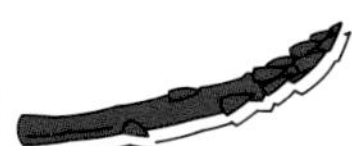

MINI BROCCOLI PIZZAS

2 cups	**(*500 mL*) small broccoli flowerets**
½ cup	**(*125 mL*) sweet red pepper cut in strips**
1 can	**CAMPBELL'S condensed Cream of Broccoli *or* Cream of Mushroom Soup**
¼ tsp	**(*1 mL*) garlic powder**
¼ tsp	**(*1 mL*) dried Italian seasoning, crushed**
6	**English muffins, split and toasted**
2 cups	**(*500 mL*) shredded mozzarella cheese (8 oz / *225 g*)**

■ Preheat oven to 375 °F (*190 °C*). Meanwhile, in small saucepan over high heat, in boiling water, cook broccoli and red pepper 3 minutes. Drain well; set aside.

■ In small bowl, combine soup, garlic and Italian seasoning. Spread soup mixture evenly over 12 muffin halves; place on cookie sheets.

■ Top each with cooked broccoli and red pepper. Sprinkle with cheese. Bake 10 minutes or until cheese melts. Serve immediately.

TIP: These individual broccoli pizzas are easy to assemble. Choose from a variety of toppers such as: sliced pepperoni, chopped artichoke hearts, chopped shrimp, sliced green onions (spring onions) and sliced olives.

Makes 12 mini pizzas.

MUSTARD CHICKEN BITES

1 can	**CAMPBELL'S condensed Cream of Chicken Soup**
2 tbsp	**(*30 mL*) Dijon-style mustard**
1 tbsp	**(*15 mL*) chopped fresh dill *or* ½ tsp (*2 mL*) dried dill weed, crushed**
1 tsp	**(*5 mL*) lemon juice**
2	**cloves garlic, minced**
1½ lb	**(*675 g*) skinless, boneless chicken breasts, cut into 1¼-inch (*3 cm*) cubes**
¼ cup	**(*50 mL*) milk**
	Fresh dill *and* lemon slices for garnish

■ In large bowl, stir together soup, mustard, dill, lemon juice and garlic. Reserve ½ cup (*125 mL*) of soup mixture for dipping sauce. Add chicken to remaining soup mixture; toss to coat well. Cover; refrigerate 2 hours.

■ On skewers, thread chicken. Place skewers on grill 6 inches (*15 cm*) above glowing coals. Grill 8 minutes or until chicken is no longer pink and golden brown, turning often. Remove chicken from skewers. Arrange chicken on serving platter; keep warm.

■ Meanwhile, in 1-quart (*1 L*) saucepan over medium heat, stir together reserved soup mixture and milk; heat through. Serve as dipping sauce with grilled chicken. Garnish with dill and lemon, if desired.

To broil: Prepare recipe as directed above. On rack in broiler pan, place skewers. Broil 6 inches (*15 cm*) from heat 10 minutes or until chicken is no longer pink and golden brown, turning often.

Makes about 50 appetizers.

1 In large bowl, stir together soup, mustard, dill, lemon juice and garlic.

MUSTARD CHICKEN BITES

2 Add chicken to remaining soup mixture.

3 Thread chicken on skewers.

4 Turn chicken skewers to brown all sides.

CRAB PARMESAN TOASTS

CRAB PARMESAN TOASTS

1 can	**CAMPBELL'S condensed Cream of Mushroom Soup**
1 lb	**(*450 g*) (about 3 cups / *750 mL*) lump crabmeat, flaked**
½ cup	**(*125 mL*) chopped celery**
¼ cup	**(*50 mL*) sliced green onions (spring onions)**
⅛ tsp	**(*0,5 mL*) grated lemon peel**
1 tbsp	**(*15 mL*) lemon juice**
1 loaf	**French bread (about 16 inches / *40 cm*) long**
½ cup	**(*125 mL*) grated Parmesan cheese**
	Paprika

■ In medium bowl, stir together soup, crabmeat, celery, onions, lemon peel and lemon juice.

■ Diagonally slice bread into 26 slices. Arrange on 2 cookie sheets. Broil 4 inches (*10 cm*) from heat 2 minutes, turning once, until toasted.

■ Spread 2 tablespoons (*30 mL*) crab mixture on *each* bread slice. Sprinkle with Parmesan and paprika.

■ Broil 5 minutes or until lightly browned. Serve immediately.

Makes 26 appetizers.

BARBECUE PORK POTATO TOPPER

1 tbsp	**(*15 mL*) vegetable oil**
1	**medium onion, thinly sliced**
½ lb	**(*225 g*) boneless pork, cut into very thin strips**
1 can	**CAMPBELL'S condensed Tomato Soup**
2 tbsp	**(*30 mL*) water**
1 tbsp	**(*15 mL*) brown sugar**
1 tbsp	**(*15 mL*) vinegar**
2 tsp	**(*10 mL*) Worcestershire sauce**
4	**hot baked potatoes, split**

■ In 10-inch (*25 cm*) skillet over medium heat, in hot oil, cook onion until golden brown and tender. Push onions to one side, add pork; cook until browned. Spoon off fat.

■ Stir in soup, water, sugar, vinegar and Worcestershire sauce. Cook 5 minutes. Spoon mixture over potatoes.

Makes about 2½ cups (625 mL) or 4 servings.

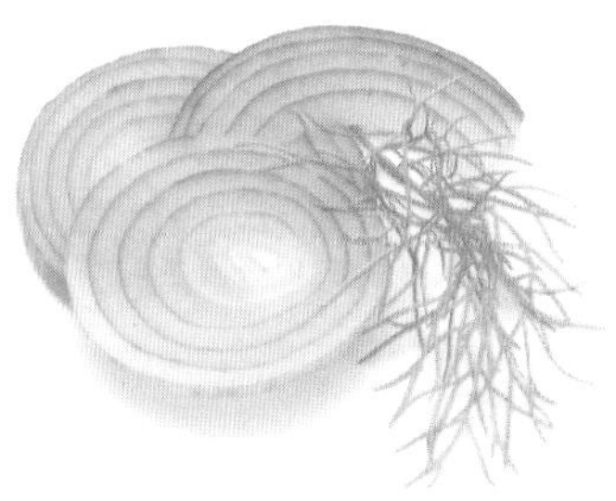

Fajita-Style Beef Potato Topper

1 tbsp	***(15 mL)*** **vegetable oil**
1	**medium onion, cut into wedges**
½ cup	***(125 mL)*** **green pepper cut in 2-inch (*5 cm*) long strips**
½ lb	***(225 g)*** **boneless beef round steak, cut into very thin strips**
1 can	**CAMPBELL'S condensed Cream of Mushroom Soup**
¼ cup	***(50 mL)*** **water**
2 tsp	***(10 mL)*** **lime juice**
½ tsp	***(2 mL)*** **dried oregano leaves, crushed**
¼ tsp	***(1 mL)*** **ground cumin**
4	**hot baked potatoes, split**
	Salsa *or* taco sauce

■ In 10-inch (*25 cm*) skillet over medium heat, in hot oil, cook onion and green pepper until vegetables are browned and tender. Push vegetables to one side, add beef; cook until browned. Spoon off fat.

■ Stir in soup, water, lime juice, oregano and cumin. Heat through, stirring occasionally. Spoon mixture over potatoes. Top with salsa.

Makes about 3 cups (750 mL) or 4 servings.

SHRIMP STUFFED MUSHROOMS

1 can	**CAMPBELL'S condensed Cream of Mushroom Soup**
½ lb	**(*225 g*) deveined shelled shrimp, cooked and chopped**
⅓ cup	**(*75 mL*) grated Parmesan cheese**
⅓ cup	**(*75 mL*) dry bread crumbs**
¼ cup	**(*50 mL*) finely chopped celery**
¼ cup	**(*50 mL*) finely chopped green onions (spring onions)**
2 tbsp	**(*30 mL*) prepared horseradish**
2 tbsp	**(*30 mL*) chili sauce**
40	**large fresh mushrooms (about 2½ lb / *1 kg*)**
2 tbsp	**(*30 mL*) margarine *or* butter, melted**

■ *To prepare stuffing:* In medium bowl, combine soup, shrimp, Parmesan, bread crumbs, celery, onions, horseradish and chili sauce until well blended.

■ Remove stems from mushrooms; reserve stems for another use.

■ Lightly brush mushroom caps with melted margarine; arrange on rack in broiler pan. Spoon about *1 tablespoon* (*15 mL*) stuffing into *each* mushroom cap.

■ Broil 4 inches (*10 cm*) from heat 4 minutes or until hot.

Shrimp Stuffed Mushrooms and Tomatoes: Prepare Shrimp Stuffed Mushrooms as directed above, *except* substitute *30 cherry tomatoes* for 20 mushrooms. Slice tops off tomatoes; scoop out seeds and drain inverted on paper towels. Spoon about *2 teaspoons* (*10 mL*) stuffing into *each* tomato. Broil as directed above.

Makes 40 appetizers.

Herb Cheesecake

3 pkgs (8 oz *each*)	**(*700 g*) cream cheese, softened**
2 cups	**(*500 mL*) sour cream, divided**
1 can	**CAMPBELL'S condensed Cream of Celery Soup**
3	**eggs**
½ cup	**(*125 mL*) grated Romano *or* Asiago cheese**
2	**cloves garlic, minced**
1 tbsp	**(*15 mL*) cornstarch (cornflour)**
2 tbsp	**(*30 mL*) finely chopped fresh basil leaves *or* 2 tsp (*10 mL*) dried basil leaves, crushed**
1 tbsp	**(*15 mL*) finely chopped thyme leaves *or* 1 tsp (*5 mL*) dried thyme leaves, crushed**
1 tsp	**(*5 mL*) finely chopped fresh tarragon leaves *or* ¼ tsp (*1 mL*) dried tarragon leaves, crushed**
½ tsp	**(*2 mL*) cracked pepper**
	Sweet red pepper strips, lemon peel twists *and* assorted fresh herbs for garnish
	Crackers, melba toast *or* fresh cut-up vegetables

■ Preheat oven to 350 °F (*180 °C*). Grease side and bottom of 9-inch (*23 cm*) springform pan.

■ In food processor* or large mixer bowl, combine cream cheese, *1 cup* (*250 mL*) of sour cream, and soup. Blend mixture in food processor or beat with electric mixer at medium speed, until smooth. Add eggs, Romano cheese, garlic, cornstarch, basil, thyme, tarragon and pepper. Blend or beat until smooth. Turn into prepared pan and place on jelly-roll pan.

■ Bake 1 hour or until light brown (top may crack). Turn off oven; let stand in oven 30 minutes more. Cool in pan on wire rack. Cover; refrigerate until serving time, at least 4 hours or overnight.

■ Spread remaining 1 cup (*250 mL*) sour cream over cheesecake. Garnish with red pepper, lemon twists and assorted fresh herbs, if desired. Serve with crackers.

** Quantity of mixture requires an 8-cup (2 L) capacity food processor.*

Makes 16 appetizer servings.

HERB CHEESECAKE

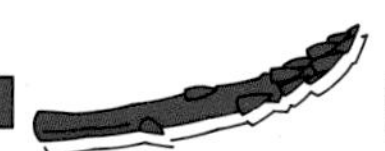

FLORENTINE PARTY APPETIZERS

4	**eggs, beaten**
1 can	**CAMPBELL'S condensed Cream of Mushroom Soup**
1 cup	**(*250 mL*) sharp Cheddar cold-pack cheese spread, at room temperature**
2 pkgs (10 oz *each*)	**(*570 g*) frozen chopped spinach, thawed, *well drained* and finely chopped**
½ cup	**(*125 mL*) chopped water chestnuts**
¼ cup	**(*50 mL*) finely chopped green onions (spring onions)**
1 pkg (8 oz)	**(*235 g*) refrigerated crescent rolls***
3 tbsp	**(*45 mL*) diced pimento**

■ In large bowl, combine eggs, soup and cheese spread. Stir in spinach, water chestnuts and green onions; mix well.

■ Unroll crescent rolls, but *do not separate.* Press onto bottom of 13- by 9-inch (*33 x 23 cm*) greased baking pan. Gently press seams together. Spread spinach mixture over dough. Top with pimento.

■ Bake at 350 °F (*180 °C*) for 40 minutes or until knife inserted in center comes out clean. Let stand 10 minutes before cutting. Cut into 1½-inch (*4 cm*) pieces.

** If not available at your food market, omit refrigerated crescent rolls and spoon spinach mixture onto bottom of well greased 13- by 9-inch (33 X 23 cm) baking pan.*

Makes 40 appetizers.

1 Add spinach, water chestnuts and green onions to soup-cheese mixture; mix well.

2 Press crescent rolls, without separating, onto bottom of greased baking pan.

3 Spread spinach mixture over dough and top with pimento.

FLORENTINE PARTY APPETIZERS

PIZZA POTATO TOPPER

1 tbsp	**(*15 mL*) vegetable oil**
1 cup	**(*250 mL*) chopped green pepper**
½ tsp	**(*2 mL*) dried basil leaves, crushed**
½ tsp	**(*2 mL*) dried oregano leaves, crushed**
1 can	**CAMPBELL'S condensed Tomato Soup**
2 tbsp	**(*30 mL*) water**
½ cup	**(*125 mL*) pepperoni slices cut in half**
4	**hot baked potatoes, split**
	Shredded mozzarella cheese

■ In 1½-quart (*1,5 L*) saucepan over medium heat, in hot oil, cook pepper, basil and oregano until pepper is tender. Stir in soup, water and pepperoni. Heat through, stirring occasionally.

■ Spoon mixture over potatoes. Top with cheese.

To microwave: In 1½-quart (*1,5 L*) microwave-safe casserole, combine oil, pepper, basil and oregano. Cover with lid; microwave on HIGH 4 minutes or until pepper is tender, stirring halfway through cooking. Stir in soup, water and pepperoni. Cover; microwave on HIGH 3 minutes or until hot. Continue as directed above.

Makes about 2 cups (500 mL) or 4 servings.

STROGANOFF POTATO TOPPER

1 lb	**(*450 g*) ground beef**
½ cup	**(*125 mL*) chopped onion**
1	**clove garlic, minced**
1 can	**CAMPBELL'S condensed Cream of Mushroom Soup**
½ tsp	**(*2 mL*) paprika**
½ cup	**(*125 mL*) sour cream**
6	**hot baked potatoes, split**
	Chopped tomato
	Chopped fresh parsley

■ In 10-inch (*25 cm*) skillet, over medium heat, cook beef, onion and garlic until onion is tender and beef is browned and no longer pink. Spoon off fat. Stir in soup and paprika. Heat through, stirring occasionally. Remove from heat. Stir in sour cream.

■ Spoon mixture over potatoes. Top with chopped tomato and parsley.

To microwave: In 2-quart (*2 L*) microwave-safe casserole, combine onion and garlic. Cover with lid; microwave on HIGH 2 minutes, stirring halfway through cooking. Crumble beef in casserole. Cover; microwave on HIGH 5 minutes or until beef is no longer pink, stirring halfway through cooking. Spoon off fat. Stir in soup and paprika. Cover; microwave on HIGH 3 minutes. Stir in sour cream. Continue as directed above.

Makes about 3 cups (750 mL) or 6 servings.

SUMMER GARDEN SOUP

1 can	**CAMPBELL's condensed Chicken Broth**
⅔ cup	**(*150 mL*) water**
½ cup	**(*125 mL*) zucchini cut in 2-inch (*5 cm*) matchstick-thin strips**
½ cup	**(*125 mL*) seeded and chopped tomato**
½ cup	**(*125 mL*) frozen whole kernel corn (sweet corn)**
⅓ cup	**(*75 mL*) chopped carrot**
¼ cup	**(*50 mL*) chopped onion**
1½ tsp	**(*7 mL*) chopped fresh basil leaves *or* ½ tsp (*2 mL*) dried basil leaves, crushed**

■ In 2-quart (*2 L*) saucepan over high heat, combine broth, water, zucchini, tomato, corn, carrot and onion. Heat to boiling.

■ Reduce heat to low. Cook 10 minutes or until vegetables are tender, stirring occasionally. Stir in basil.

To microwave: In 1½-quart (*1,5 L*) microwave-safe casserole, combine broth, water, zucchini, tomato, corn, carrot and onion. Cover with lid; microwave on HIGH 12 minutes or until vegetables are tender, stirring twice during cooking. Stir in basil.

Makes about 3 cups (750 mL) or 3 side-dish servings.

SOUTHWEST POTATO SOUP

1 tbsp	**(*15 mL*) margarine *or* butter**
½ cup	**(*125 mL*) chopped green onions (spring onions)**
1 can	**CAMPBELL'S condensed Cream of Potato Soup ***
1½ cups	**(*375 mL*) milk**
¼ cup	**(*50 mL*) shredded Monterey Jack cheese with jalapeño peppers** (1 oz / *30 g*)**

■ In 2-quart (*2 L*) saucepan over medium heat, in hot margarine, cook green onions until tender, stirring occasionally.

■ Add soup and milk; stir until blended. Heat through, stirring occasionally. Remove from heat. Add cheese, stirring until cheese melts.

** If not available at your food market, substitute 1 can CAMPBELL'S condensed Cream of Celery Soup and 1 medium potato, cooked, peeled and diced (⅔ cup / 150 mL).*

*** If not available at your food market, substitute ¼ cup (50 mL) shredded Monterey Jack or Cheddar cheese and 1 teaspoon (5 mL) diced canned jalapeño peppers.*

Makes about 2¾ cups (675 mL) or 3 side-dish servings.

SUMMER GARDEN SOUP

TUNA-TORTELLINI SOUP

1 can	**CAMPBELL'S condensed Cream of Broccoli *or* Cream of Chicken Soup**
1 can	**CAMPBELL's condensed Chicken Broth**
¼ tsp	**(*1 mL*) dried basil leaves, crushed**
⅛ tsp	**(*0,5 mL*) garlic powder**
2 cups	**(*500 mL*) fresh or frozen cheese-filled tortellini***
1 cup	**(*250 mL*) frozen whole kernel corn (sweet corn)**
1½ cups	**(*375 mL*) milk**
1 can (6½ oz)	**(*185 g*) tuna, drained**
2 tbsp	**(*30 mL*) diced pimento**
	Chopped fresh parsley for garnish

■ In 3-quart (*3 L*) saucepan, combine soup, broth, basil and garlic. Cover; over high heat, heat to boiling.

■ Add tortellini and corn. Reduce heat to low. Cover; cook 10 minutes or until tortellini is tender, stirring occasionally.

■ Add milk, tuna and pimento; heat through, stirring occasionally. Garnish with parsley, if desired.

** If not available at your food market, substitute 2 cups (500 mL) cooked and drained corkscrew macaroni. Add along with milk.*

Makes about 6 cups (1,5 L) or 4 main-dish servings.

MACARONI RATATOUILLE SOUP

1 lb	**(*450 g*) sweet (mild) Italian sausage, casing removed**
1	**medium onion, chopped**
2	**cloves garlic, minced**
½ tsp	**(*2 mL*) dried oregano leaves, crushed**
1 can	**CAMPBELL'S condensed Tomato Soup**
1 can	**CAMPBELL'S condensed Beef Broth ***
1 can (about 8 oz)	**(*225 mL*) tomatoes, undrained and cut up**
2 cups	**(*500 mL*) water**
1 lb	**(*450 g*) eggplant, cut into ½-inch (*1 cm*) pieces**
½ tsp	**(*2 mL*) pepper**
½ cup	**(*125 mL*) *uncooked* elbow macaroni**
	Chopped fresh parsley *and* grated Parmesan cheese for garnish

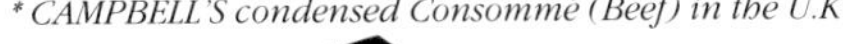
** CAMPBELL'S condensed Consommé (Beef) in the U.K.*

■ In 5-quart (*5 L*) Dutch oven over medium heat, cook sausage, onion, garlic and oregano until sausage is browned, stirring to separate sausage. Spoon off fat.

■ Add soup, broth, undrained tomatoes, water, eggplant and pepper. Heat to boiling. Reduce heat to low. Cover; cook 15 minutes, stirring occasionally.

■ Stir in macaroni; cook 10 minutes more or until macaroni is tender, stirring occasionally. Garnish with parsley and cheese, if desired.

Makes about 7 cups (1,8 L) or 5 main-dish servings.

HAM BARLEY SOUP

3 tbsp	**(*45 mL*) margarine *or* butter**
1 cup	**(*250 mL*) sliced fresh mushrooms**
½ cup	**(*125 mL*) chopped onion**
¼ tsp	**(*1 mL*) dried thyme leaves, crushed**
⅔ cup	**(*150 mL*) regular pearl barley**
1 can	**CAMPBELL's condensed Chicken Broth**
1 can	**CAMPBELL'S condensed Beef Broth** *
1½ cups	**(*375 mL*) water**
¼ tsp	**(*1 mL*) pepper**
1½ cups	**(*375 mL*) milk**
¼ lb	**(*115 g*) cooked ham, cut into 1½-inch (*4 cm*) matchstick-thin strips (1 cup / *250 mL*)**
1 cup	**(*250 mL*) frozen peas**

** CAMPBELL'S condensed Consommé (Beef) in the U.K.*

■ In 4-quart (*4 L*) saucepan over medium heat, in hot margarine, cook mushrooms, onion and thyme 3 minutes, stirring occasionally. Add barley; cook 2 minutes or until golden, stirring often.

■ Add broths, water and pepper. Cover; heat to boiling. Reduce heat to low. Cook 40 minutes.

■ Stir in milk, ham and peas. Cook 5 minutes more or until barley is tender.

Makes about 6½ cups (1,6 L) or 4 main-dish servings.

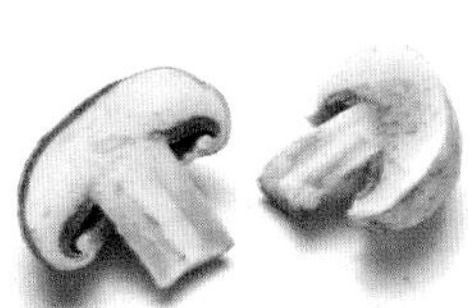

1 Cook mushrooms, onion and thyme, stirring occasionally.

2 Add barley and cook until golden.

HAM BARLEY SOUP

3 Add broths, water and pepper.

4 Stir in milk, ham and peas.

TORTILLA SOUP

1	**lime**
	Vegetable oil
½ cup	**(*125 mL*) chopped onion**
½ tsp	**(*2 mL*) ground cumin**
⅛ tsp	**(*0,5 mL*) dried oregano leaves, crushed**
1	**clove garlic, minced**
1 can	**CAMPBELL'S condensed Chicken Broth**
1 soup can	**water**
½ cup	**(*125 mL*) chopped tomato**
1 can (4 oz)	**(*110 g*) chopped green chilies**
3	**corn tortillas**
	Shredded Monterey Jack *or* Cheddar cheese
1 cup	**(*250 mL*) shredded lettuce**

■ Cut 3 thin slices from lime; set aside. Squeeze *1 teaspoon (5 mL)* juice from remaining lime; set aside.

■ In 2-quart (*2 L*) saucepan over medium heat, in 1 tablespoon (*15 mL*) hot oil, cook onion, cumin, oregano and garlic until onion is tender.

■ Add broth, water, tomato, chilies and reserved lime juice. Heat to boiling. Reduce heat to low; cook 10 minutes.

■ Meanwhile, cut tortillas into thin strips. In 10-inch (*25 cm*) skillet, heat *½ inch* (*1 cm*) oil to 375 °F (*190 °C*). Fry tortilla strips, a few at a time, until crisp. Remove to paper towels to drain.

■ Place several tortilla strips in 3 bowls. Ladle soup into bowls; sprinkle with cheese. Top with reserved lime slices and lettuce. Serve immediately.

TIP: Substitute tortilla chips or crumbled taco shells for corn tortilla strips.

Makes about 3½ cups (875 mL) or 3 side-dish servings.

TORTILLA SOUP

SOUTH-OF-THE-BORDER ONION SOUP

1 can	**CAMPBELL'S condensed French Onion Soup** *
1 soup can	**water**
½ cup	**(*125 mL*) whole kernel corn (sweet corn)**
½ cup	**(*125 mL*) chopped tomato**
2 tbsp	**(*30 mL*) chopped green chilies**
1 tbsp	**(*15 mL*) lime juice**
¼ tsp	**(*1 mL*) ground cumin**

** Not available in the U.K.*

■ In 2-quart (*2 L*) saucepan, combine soup, water, corn, tomato, chilies, lime juice and cumin. Over medium heat, heat to boiling.

■ Reduce heat to low. Cook 10 minutes.

Makes about 4 cups (1 L) or 4 side-dish servings.

DOWN-HOME VEGETABLE CHOWDER

2 tbsp	**(*30 mL*) margarine *or* butter**
½ cup	**(*125 mL*) sliced celery**
¼ cup	**(*50 mL*) sliced green onions (spring onions)**
1 can	**CAMPBELL'S condensed Cream of Potato Soup** *
1 soup can	**milk**
1 cup	**(*250 mL*) frozen whole kernel corn (sweet corn)**
⅛ tsp	**(*0,5 mL*) pepper**

In 2-quart (*2 L*) saucepan over medium heat, in hot margarine, cook celery and green onions until tender, stirring occasionally. Add soup, milk, corn and pepper. Heat through, stirring often.

TIP: For added flavor, sprinkle crumbled cooked bacon, chopped green onion tops and chopped sweet red pepper on each serving.

** If not available at your food market, substitute 1 can CAMPBELL'S condensed Cream of Celery Soup and 1 medium potato, cooked, peeled and diced (⅔ cup / 150 mL).*

Makes about 3½ cups (875 mL) or 3 side-dish servings.

CREAMY SHRIMP BISQUE

2 tbsp (*30 mL*) **margarine** *or* **butter**

1 cup (*250 mL*) **sliced fresh mushrooms**

2 tbsp (*30 mL*) **sliced green onion (spring onion)**

1 **clove garlic, minced**

1 can **CAMPBELL's condensed Chicken Broth**

1 lb (*450 g*) **frozen shelled and deveined medium shrimp**

3 tbsp (*45 mL*) **all-purpose flour**

½ cup (*125 mL*) **light cream**

⅓ cup (*75 mL*) **Chablis** *or* **other dry white wine**

1 tbsp (*15 mL*) **chopped fresh parsley**

■ In 10-inch (*25 cm*) skillet over medium heat, in hot margarine, cook mushrooms, green onion and garlic until tender, stirring occasionally. Add broth and shrimp. Heat to boiling.

■ Meanwhile, in cup, stir together flour and cream until well blended. Stir into broth mixture. Cook until mixture boils and thickens, stirring often.

■ Add wine; heat through, stirring occasionally. Sprinkle with parsley.

Makes about 4 cups (1 L) or 4 main-dish servings.

HEARTY OYSTER CHOWDER

8 oz	**(*225 g*) shucked oysters**
	Milk
¼ cup	**(*50 mL*) margarine *or* butter**
2	**large carrots, sliced**
1	**large onion, chopped**
1	**large potato, peeled and cut into ½-inch (*1 cm*) chunks**
1 can	**CAMPBELL'S condensed Cream of Celery *or* Cream of Chicken Soup**
¼ cup	**(*50 mL*) chopped fresh parsley**
¼ tsp	**(*1 mL*) pepper**

■ Drain oysters, reserving liquid. Coarsely chop oysters; set aside. In 2-cup (*500 mL*) measure, add milk to oyster liquid to make 1½ cups (*375 mL*) liquid total; set aside.

■ In 3-quart (*3 L*) saucepan over medium heat, in hot margarine, cook carrots, onion and potato until vegetables are tender, stirring often. Add oysters. Cook 1 minute.

■ Add soup, milk mixture, parsley and pepper. Heat through until oysters are done, stirring occasionally. *Do not boil.*

Makes about 5½ cups (1,4 L) or 5 side-dish servings.

SAVORY PORK STEW

2 tbsp	**(*30 mL*) vegetable oil**
1 lb	**(*450 g*) boneless pork shoulder, cut into ¾-inch (*2 cm*) pieces**
2 cans	**CAMPBELL'S condensed Cream of Celery Soup**
1½ cups	**(*375 mL*) apple juice**
¼ tsp	**(*1 mL*) pepper**
¼ tsp	**(*1 mL*) caraway seed**
2	**medium red potatoes, cut into chunks**
3	**carrots, diagonally sliced**
3 cups	**(*750 mL*) coarsely chopped cabbage**
½ cup	**(*125 mL*) milk**

■ In 4-quart (*4 L*) saucepan over medium heat, in hot oil, cook pork until browned on all sides.

■ Add soup, juice, pepper and caraway. Heat to boiling. Reduce heat to low. Cover; cook 30 minutes, stirring occasionally.

■ Add potatoes and carrots. Cover; cook 10 minutes. Add cabbage. Cover; cook 15 minutes or until vegetables are tender.

■ Add milk. Heat through, stirring occasionally. *Do not boil.*

Makes about 8 cups (2 L) or 6 main-dish servings.

BUTTERNUT SQUASH BISQUE

4 cups	**(*1 L*) cubed, seeded, peeled butternut squash**
2 tbsp	**(*30 mL*) margarine *or* butter**
1	**large onion, finely chopped**
1	**clove garlic, minced**
1 can	**CAMPBELL'S condensed Chicken Broth**
¼ tsp	**(*1 mL*) salt**
¼ tsp	**(*1 mL*) pepper**
⅛ tsp	**(*0,5 mL*) ground nutmeg**
½ cup	**(*125 mL*) heavy cream**
	Chopped fresh parsley for garnish

■ In 3-quart (*3 L*) saucepan, place squash; add water to cover squash. Heat to boiling. Reduce heat to low. Cover; cook 10 minutes or until squash is tender. Drain. In covered blender or food processor, blend squash until smooth.

■ In same saucepan over medium heat, in hot margarine, cook onion and garlic until tender, stirring occasionally. Add puréed squash, broth, salt, pepper and nutmeg. Heat to boiling. Reduce heat to low; cook 5 minutes.

■ Stir in heavy cream. Heat through, stirring occasionally. If necessary, thin to desired consistency with milk or water. Heat through. Garnish with parsley, if desired.

Makes about 4 cups (1 L) or 5 side-dish servings.

1 Cook squash in water until tender.

BUTTERNUT SQUASH BISQUE

2 Drain squash, then blend in food processor.

3 Add puréed squash to cooked onion and garlic mixture.

4 Stir in cream and mix well.

CREAMY CHICKEN-BROCCOLI SOUP

CREAMY CHICKEN-BROCCOLI SOUP

2 tbsp	**(*30 mL*) margarine *or* butter**
1 cup	**(*250 mL*) sliced fresh mushrooms**
½ cup	**(*125 mL*) chopped onion**
½ cup	**(*125 mL*) green *or* sweet red pepper cut in 1-inch (*2,5 cm*) strips**
1	**clove garlic, minced**
½ tsp	**(*2 mL*) dried basil leaves, crushed**
1 can	**CAMPBELL'S condensed Cream of Chicken *or* Cream of Broccoli Soup**
1 can	**CAMPBELL'S condensed Chicken Broth**
1¾ cups	**(*425 mL*) milk**
1½ cups	**(*375 mL*) cut-up cooked chicken**
⅛ tsp	**(*0,5 mL*) black pepper**
	Generous dash ground nutmeg
1 cup	**(*250 mL*) broccoli flowerets**

■ In 3-quart (*3 L*) saucepan over medium heat, in hot margarine, cook mushrooms, onion, green pepper, garlic and basil until vegetables are tender, stirring occasionally.

■ Stir in soup and broth until smooth. Stir in milk, chicken, black pepper and nutmeg. Add broccoli; heat to boiling. Reduce heat to low. Cover; cook 5 minutes or until broccoli is tender.

Makes about 6 cups (1,5 L) or 4 main-dish servings.

TOMATO FRENCH ONION SOUP

1 can	**CAMPBELL'S condensed Tomato Soup**
1 can	**CAMPBELL'S condensed French Onion Soup** *
2 soup cans	**water**
	Toasted bread quarters *or* croutons
	Grated Parmesan cheese
	Fresh thyme sprigs for garnish

** Not available in the U.K.*

■ In 2-quart (*2 L*) saucepan, combine tomato soup and onion soup. Add water. Over medium heat, heat through, stirring occasionally.

■ Top each bowl of soup with bread and Parmesan cheese. Garnish with thyme, if desired.

Makes about 5 cups (1,2 L) or 5 side-dish servings.

TOMATO DILL SOUP

1 can	**CAMPBELL'S condensed Tomato Soup**
1 soup can	**milk *or* half-and-half**
¼ tsp	**(*1 mL*) dried dill weed, crushed**
	Sour cream

In 1½-quart (*1,5 L*) saucepan, stir soup. Gradually add milk. Add dill. Over medium heat, heat through, stirring occasionally. Serve with sour cream.

To microwave: In 1½-quart (*1,5 L*) microwave-safe casserole, stir soup. Gradually add milk. Add dill. Cover with lid; microwave on HIGH 6 minutes, stirring once during cooking. Serve with sour cream.

Makes about 3 cups (750 mL) or 3 side-dish servings.

TOMATO BEEF STEW

½ lb	**(*225 g*) ground beef**
1 can	**CAMPBELL'S condensed Tomato Soup**
½ soup can	**water**
1 cup	**(*250 mL*) frozen cut green beans**
½ cup	**(*125 mL*) frozen sliced carrots**
1 tsp	**(*5 mL*) Worcestershire sauce**

■ In 1½-quart (*1,5 L*) saucepan over medium heat, cook beef until browned and no longer pink, stirring to separate meat. Spoon off fat.

■ Stir in soup and water. Add beans, carrots and Worcestershire sauce. Heat to simmering. Cook 10 minutes or until vegetables are tender, stirring occasionally.

Garden Vegetable Beef Stew: Prepare Tomato Beef Stew as directed above, *except* substitute 1½ cups (*375 mL*) *frozen mixed vegetables* for the green beans and carrots. Add vegetables as directed above.

Makes about 3 cups (750 mL) or 2 main-dish servings.

SPEEDY SPICY CHILI

1 lb	**(*450 g*) ground beef**
½ cup	**(*125 mL*) chopped onion**
1	**clove garlic, minced**
1 tbsp	**(*15 mL*) chili powder**
1 can (16 oz)	**(*450 mL*) pork and beans in tomato sauce**
1 can	**CAMPBELL'S condensed Tomato Soup**
1 can (4 oz)	**(*110 g*) chopped green chilies**
½ cup	**(*125 mL*) water**
	Sliced green onion *or* spring onion *and* sour cream for garnish

■ In 10-inch (*25 cm*) skillet over medium-high heat, cook beef, onion, garlic and chili powder until beef is browned and onion is tender, stirring to separate meat. Spoon off fat.

■ Add beans, soup, chilies and water. Heat to boiling. Reduce heat to low. Cook 10 minutes, stirring occasionally. Garnish with onion and sour cream, if desired.

TIP: Pass bowls of chopped tomato, shredded cheese, sliced green onions and sour cream to add pizzazz to this extra-fast chili.

Makes about 4 cups (1 L) or 4 main-dish servings.

CINCINNATI CHILI

1 lb	**(*450 g*) ground beef**
1 cup	**(*250 mL*) chopped green pepper**
½ cup	**(*125 mL*) chopped onion**
3 tbsp	**(*45 mL*) chili powder**
2	**cloves garlic, minced**
2 cans	**CAMPBELL'S condensed Tomato Soup**
1 can (15 oz)	**(*425 mL*) kidney beans, undrained**
1 tbsp	**(*15 mL*) vinegar**
¼ tsp	**(*1 mL*) ground cinnamon**
	Hot cooked spaghetti
	Shredded Cheddar cheese for garnish

■ In 4-quart (*4 L*) saucepan over medium heat, cook beef, green pepper, onion, chili powder and garlic until beef is browned and vegetables are tender, stirring to separate meat. Spoon off fat.

■ Add soup, undrained kidney beans, vinegar and cinnamon. Heat to boiling. Reduce heat to low. Cook 15 minutes, stirring occasionally.

■ Serve over spaghetti. Sprinkle with cheese, if desired.

Makes about 6 cups (1,5 L) chili or 5 main-dish servings.

SPEEDY SPICY CHILI (top)
CINCINNATI CHILI (bottom)

COUNTRY CHICKEN STEW

2	**slices bacon, diced**
1	**medium onion, sliced**
1 tsp	**(*5 mL*) dried oregano leaves, crushed**
1 can	**CAMPBELL'S condensed Cream of Chicken Soup**
1 soup can	**water**
4	**medium potatoes, peeled and cut into chunks**
2	**medium carrots, diagonally sliced**
1 cup	**(*250 mL*) frozen cut green beans**
1½ cups	**(*375 mL*) cubed cooked chicken**
2 tbsp	**(*30 mL*) chopped fresh parsley**

■ In 3-quart (*3 L*) saucepan over medium heat, cook bacon until crisp. Transfer to paper towels to drain, reserving drippings; set aside.

■ In hot drippings, cook onion and oregano until onion is tender.

■ Add soup, water, potatoes and carrots; heat to boiling, stirring occasionally. Reduce heat to low. Cover; cook 15 minutes, stirring mixture occasionally.

■ Stir in beans. Cover; cook 10 minutes. Stir in reserved bacon and chicken; heat through. Sprinkle with parsley.

Makes about 5½ cups (1,4 L) or 4 main-dish servings.

1 Cook bacon until crisp.

2 Cook onion and oregano in hot drippings.

COUNTRY CHICKEN STEW

3 Stir in soup, water, potatoes and carrots; cook 15 minutes.

4 Stir in beans. Cover; cook 10 minutes.

BROCCOLI FISH CHOWDER

3 tbsp	**(*45 mL*) margarine *or* butter**
1 cup	**(*250 mL*) sliced celery**
1 cup	**(*250 mL*) chopped onion**
2	**cloves garlic, minced**
¼ cup	**(*50 mL*) Chablis *or* other dry white wine**
2 cans	**CAMPBELL'S condensed Cream of Broccoli *or* Cream of Chicken Soup**
2 cups	**(*500 mL*) milk**
1 lb	**(*450 g*) firm white fish fillets, cut into 1-inch (*2,5 cm*) pieces**
2 tbsp	**(*30 mL*) diced pimento**
	Generous dash ground red pepper (cayenne)

■ In 3-quart (*3 L*) saucepan over medium heat, in hot margarine, cook celery, onion and garlic until tender, stirring often.

■ Add wine; cook 2 minutes. Add soup; stir until smooth. Gradually stir in milk. Add fish, pimento and pepper. Heat to boiling. Reduce heat to low. Cover; cook 5 minutes or until fish flakes easily when tested with fork.

TIP: Use haddock, halibut or cod in this vegetable chowder.

Makes about 6 cups (1,5 L) or 4 main-dish servings.

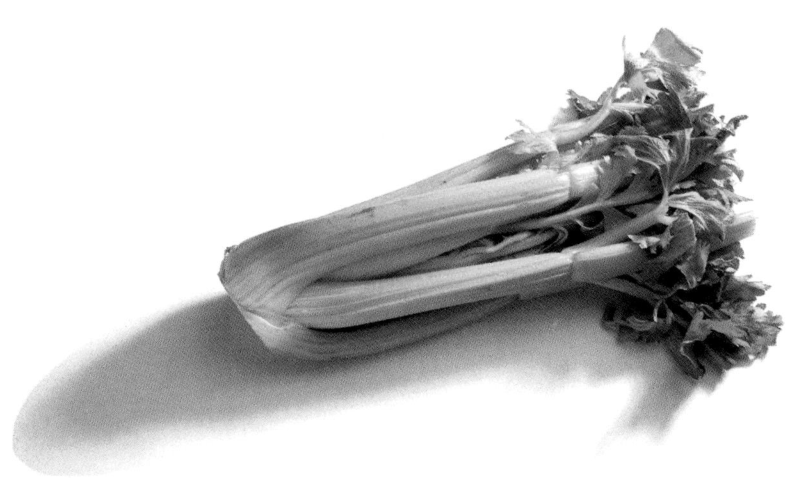

BROCCOLI FISH CHOWDER

SMOKED TURKEY BEAN SOUP

1 tbsp	**(*15 mL*) vegetable oil**
1	**medium onion, chopped**
2	**cloves garlic, minced**
1 can	**CAMPBELL'S condensed Cream of Potato *or* Cream of Chicken Soup**
1 can (about 16 oz)	**(*450 mL*) white cannellini *or* white kidney beans, drained**
1 soup can	**water**
¼ lb	**(*115 g*) smoked turkey breast, cut into ½-inch (*1 cm*) pieces (about 1 cup / *250 mL*)**
1 tsp	**(*5 mL*) paprika**
1 tbsp	**(*15 mL*) chopped fresh parsley**

■ In 2-quart (*2 L*) saucepan over medium heat, in hot oil, cook onion and garlic until tender, stirring occasionally.

■ Stir in soup, beans, water, turkey and paprika. Heat to boiling. Reduce heat to low. Cook 5 minutes. Stir in parsley. Garnish with fresh *parsley sprig*, if desired.

TIP: You can substitute leftover roast turkey or baked ham for the smoked turkey.

Makes about 4½ cups (1,1 L) or 3 main-dish servings.

HINT-OF-MINT PEA SOUP

1 can	**CAMPBELL'S condensed Cream of Potato Soup** *
1 can	**CAMPBELL'S condensed Chicken Broth**
1 pkg (10 oz)	**(*285 g*) frozen peas (2 cups / *500 mL*)**
1 tbsp	**(*15 mL*) lemon juice**
¾ tsp	**(*3 mL*) chopped fresh mint leaves *or* ¼ tsp (*1 mL*) dried mint leaves, crushed**
⅛ tsp	**(*0,5 mL*) ground white pepper**
½ cup	**(*125 mL*) milk**
	Fresh mint leaves *and* walnuts for garnish

■ In 2-quart (*2 L*) saucepan, stir soup and broth until smooth. Add peas. Over medium heat, heat to boiling, stirring occasionally. Reduce heat to low. Cover; cook 8 minutes or until peas are tender.

■ In covered blender or food processor, blend soup mixture, lemon juice, ¾ teaspoon (*3 mL*) fresh mint and pepper until smooth. Return mixture to saucepan.

■ Gradually stir in milk. Over medium heat, heat through, stirring occasionally. Garnish with fresh mint and walnuts, if desired.

** If not available at your food market, substitute one can CAMPBELL'S condensed Cream of Celery Soup and add 1 medium potato, cooked, peeled and diced (⅔ cup / 150 mL).*

Makes about 4 cups (1 L) or 4 side-dish servings.

SHORTCUT BRUNSWICK STEW

2 slices	**bacon**
½ cup	**(*125 mL*) chopped onion**
1 can	**CAMPBELL'S condensed Tomato Soup**
1 soup can	**water**
1 tsp	**(*5 mL*) Worcestershire sauce**
	Generous dash pepper
1 pkg (10 oz)	**(*285 g*) frozen lima beans (2 cups / *500 mL*)**
1 pkg (10 oz)	**(*285 g*) frozen whole kernel corn *or* sweet corn (2 cups / *500 mL*)**
2 cups	**(*500 mL*) cubed cooked chicken**

■ In 3-quart (*3 L*) saucepan over low heat, cook bacon until crisp. Transfer to paper towels to drain, reserving *1 tablespoon* (*15 mL*) drippings in pan. Crumble bacon; set aside.

■ Over medium heat, in hot drippings, cook onion until tender, stirring occasionally.

■ Stir in soup, water, Worcestershire and pepper. Heat to boiling. Add lima beans and corn. Return to boiling. Stir to separate vegetables. Reduce heat to low. Cover; cook 20 minutes, stirring occasionally.

■ Stir in chicken and reserved bacon; heat through.

Makes about 6 cups (1,5 L) or 4 main-dish servings.

1 Cook onion until tender.

2 Stir in soup, water, Worcestershire and pepper.

3 Add vegetables. Mix well.

SHORTCUT BRUNSWICK STEW

4 Add chicken and bacon.

SPICY BEAN SOUP

1 tbsp	**(*15 mL*) vegetable oil**
½ cup	**(*125 mL*) chopped green pepper**
½ cup	**(*125 mL*) chopped onion**
1 can	**CAMPBELL'S condensed Tomato Soup**
1 can (19 oz)	**(*540 mL*) chick peas (garbanzo beans), drained**
1 can (16 oz)	**(*450 mL*) black beans *or* kidney beans, drained**
1 soup can	**water**
1 tsp	**(*5 mL*) Worcestershire sauce**
⅛ tsp	**(*0,5 mL*) hot pepper sauce**
1 cup	**(*250 mL*) shredded Cheddar *or* Monterey Jack cheese (4 oz / *120 g*)**

■ In 3-quart (*3 L*) saucepan over medium heat, in hot oil, cook green pepper and onion 5 minutes, stirring occasionally.

■ Add soup, chick peas, beans, water, Worcestershire and hot pepper sauce. Heat to boiling, stirring occasionally. Reduce heat to low. Cover; cook 5 minutes. Serve topped with cheese.

TIP: Serve this hearty vegetable soup with tortilla chips, warm flour tortillas or purchased corn muffins.

Makes about 6 cups (1,5 L) or 4 side-dish servings.

SPICY BEAN SOUP

MANDARIN CHICKEN

1 can	**CAMPBELL'S condensed Chicken Broth, divided**
2 tbsp	**(*30 mL*) cornstarch (cornflour)**
¼ cup	**(*50 mL*) vinegar**
¼ cup	**(*50 mL*) sugar**
1 tbsp	**(*15 mL*) soy sauce**
½ tsp	**(*2 mL*) ground ginger**
1 can (8 oz)	**(*225 mL*) sliced water chestnuts, drained**
1 lb	**(*450 g*) skinless, boneless chicken breasts, cut into 1-inch (*2,5 cm*) chunks**
1	**small green *or* sweet red pepper, cut into strips**
1 can (11 oz)	**(*310 mL*) mandarin orange segments, drained**
	Hot cooked rice

■ In cup, stir together *¼ cup (50 mL)* of broth and the cornstarch until well blended; set aside.

■ In 10-inch *(25 cm)* skillet over medium heat, combine remaining broth, vinegar, sugar, soy sauce, ginger and water chestnuts. Heat mixture to boiling.

■ Add chicken to skillet. Reduce heat to low. Cook 10 minutes. Add green pepper; cook 3 minutes more or until chicken is no longer pink.

■ Stir in cornstarch mixture. Cook over medium heat until mixture boils and thickens, stirring constantly. Gently stir in oranges.

■ Serve over rice. Garnish with *orange peel* and fresh *parsley sprig*, if desired.

Makes about 4 cups (1 L) or 4 servings.

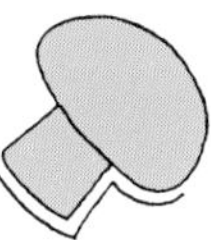

CHICKEN IN SPICY PEANUT SAUCE

6	**skinless, boneless chicken breast halves (about 1½ lb / *675 g*)**
2 tbsp	**(*30 mL*) vegetable oil**
1 can	**CAMPBELL'S condensed Cream of Chicken Soup**
3 tbsp	**(*45 mL*) chunky peanut butter**
⅔ cup	**(*150 mL*) water**
2	**green onions (spring onions), sliced**
1 tsp	**(*5 mL*) chili powder**
⅛ tsp	**(*0,5 mL*) ground red pepper (cayenne)**

■ Place chicken breasts between 2 sheets of plastic wrap. With flat side of meat mallet or rolling pin, pound to ¼-inch (*0,5 cm*) thickness.

■ In 10-inch (*25 cm*) skillet over medium heat, in hot oil, cook chicken, *half* at a time, 10 minutes or until browned on both sides. Remove chicken from skillet. Spoon off fat.

■ Add soup, peanut butter, water, onions, chili powder and pepper to skillet; stir until smooth. Heat to boiling. Return chicken to skillet. Reduce heat to low. Cover; cook 5 minutes or until chicken is no longer pink, stirring occasionally.

Makes 6 servings.

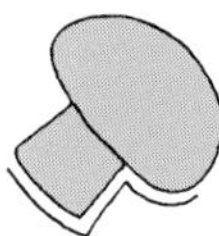

TURKEY WITH APPLE PECAN STUFFING

¼ cup	***(50 mL)*** **margarine** ***or*** **butter**
1 cup	***(250 mL)*** **chopped celery**
1 cup	***(250 mL)*** **chopped onion**
2 cans	**CAMPBELL'S condensed Chicken Broth**
1 pkg (16 oz)	***(450 g)*** **herb seasoned stuffing**
2 cups	***(500 mL)*** **chopped apples**
1 cup	***(250 mL)*** **chopped toasted pecans**
14- to 16-lb	***(6- to 7-kg)*** **ready-to-stuff turkey, cleaned**
	Apple slices for garnish

■ *To prepare stuffing:* In 4-quart (*4 L*) saucepan over medium heat, in hot margarine, cook celery and onion until tender. Add broth; heat to boiling. Remove from heat. Add stuffing, apples and pecans; toss to mix well.

■ Spoon stuffing mixture lightly into turkey neck and body cavities. Fold skin over stuffing; skewer closed. Tie legs. On rack in roasting pan, place turkey breast-side up. Insert meat thermometer into thickest part of meat between breast and thigh, not touching bone.

■ Roast, uncovered, at 325 °F (*160 °C*) for 4 hours or until internal temperature reaches 180 °F (*82 °C*) and drumstick moves easily when twisted. Baste turkey occasionally with drippings. When skin turns golden, cover loosely with tent of foil. Garnish with apple, if desired.

Makes 14 to 16 servings.

To prepare stuffing in casserole: Prepare stuffing as directed above. Spoon stuffing mixture into greased 2-quart (*2 L*) casserole. Cover; bake at 375 °F (*190 °C*) for 30 minutes or until mixture is hot.

Makes about 8 cups (2 L).

1 Cook celery and onion until tender.

2 After broth has been brought to boil, remove pan from heat. Add stuffing, apples and pecans.

TURKEY WITH APPLE PECAN STUFFING

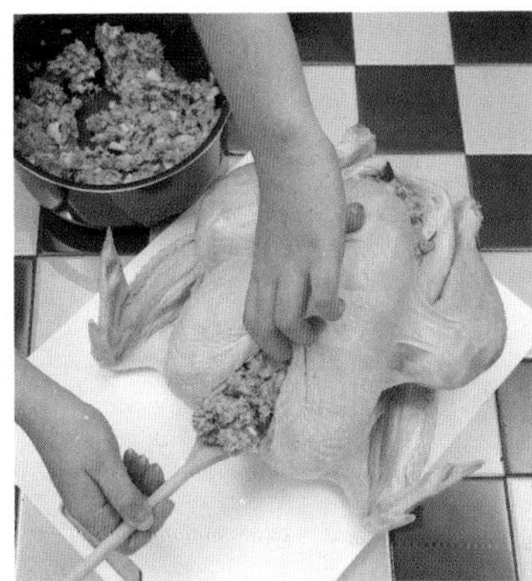

3 Spoon stuffing into turkey neck and body cavities.

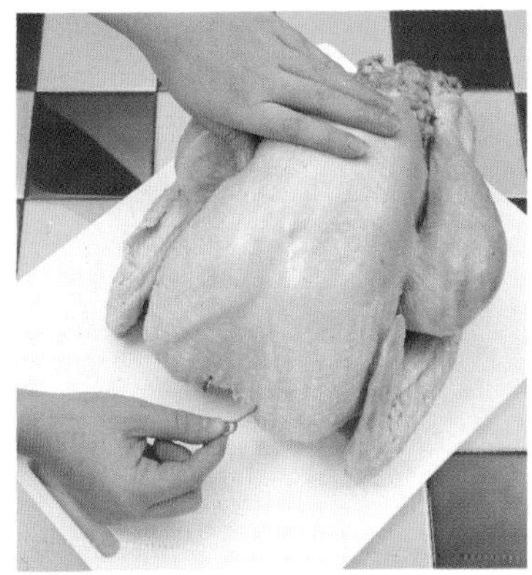

4 Fold skin over stuffing; skewer closed.

GINGER CHICKEN STIR-FRY

3 tbsp	**(*45 mL*) vegetable oil, divided**
1 lb	**(*450 g*) skinless, boneless chicken breasts *or* thighs, cut into strips**
4 cups	**(*1 L*) fresh vegetables**
1	**clove garlic, minced**
1 can	**CAMPBELL'S condensed Chicken Broth**
2 tbsp	**(*30 mL*) cornstarch (cornflour)**
1 tbsp	**(*15 mL*) soy sauce**
½ tsp	**(*2 mL*) ground ginger**
	Hot cooked noodles *or* rice
	Toasted sliced almonds

■ In 10-inch (*25 cm*) skillet or wok over medium-high heat, in *2 tablespoons* (*30 mL*) hot oil, stir-fry chicken until browned and no longer pink. Remove; set aside.

■ In same skillet in remaining 1 tablespoon (*15 mL*) oil, stir-fry vegetables and garlic until tender-crisp.

■ Meanwhile, in bowl, combine broth, cornstarch, soy sauce and ginger until smooth. Add to skillet along with reserved chicken. Cook until mixture boils and thickens, stirring constantly. Serve over noodles. Sprinkle with toasted almonds.

TIP: When stir-frying, it's easier to lift and turn the meat and vegetables if you use a long-handled spoon or spatula. Broccoli, beans, onions, sweet red pepper, snow peas and cauliflower are used to make this stir-fry which can be served over cellophane noodles. (See Tip below.)

TIP: Cellophane noodles are available in the specialty sections of most supermarkets. The *uncooked* noodles can either be cooked in boiling water, drained and used as traditional noodles, or cooked briefly in hot oil until crispy.

Makes about 4 cups (1 L) or 4 servings.

GINGER CHICKEN STIR-FRY

Country-Style Smothered Chicken

2 slices	**bacon**
2½- to 3-lb	***(1,1- to 1,4-kg)*** **broiler-fryer chicken, cut up**
1 can	**CAMPBELL'S condensed Cream of Mushroom soup**
1	**clove garlic, minced**
1 tsp	***(5 mL)*** **dried basil leaves, crushed**
1	**medium onion, sliced**
	Hot cooked rice
	Fresh basil for garnish

■ In 10-inch *(25 cm)* skillet over medium heat, cook bacon until crisp. Transfer to paper towels to drain, reserving drippings in pan. Crumble bacon; set aside.

■ Over medium heat, in hot drippings, cook chicken 10 minutes or until browned on all sides. Spoon off fat.

■ Add soup, garlic and basil; stir until smooth. Heat to boiling. Reduce heat to low. Cover; cook 20 minutes.

■ Add onion. Cover; cook 15 minutes more or until chicken is no longer pink and juices run clear, stirring occasionally. Serve over rice. Sprinkle with reserved bacon. Garnish with basil, if desired.

Makes 6 servings.

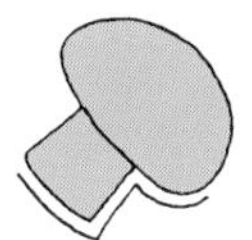

CHICKEN PASTA PARMESAN

2 tbsp	**(*30 mL*) vegetable oil**
1 lb	**(*450 g*) skinless, boneless chicken breasts, cut into cubes**
¼ cup	**(*50 mL*) chopped onion**
1 can	**CAMPBELL'S condensed Cream of Broccoli *or* Cream of Chicken Soup**
2 tbsp	**(*30 mL*) milk**
1 tbsp	**(*15 mL*) dry sherry**
1 cup	**(*250 mL*) sliced fresh mushrooms**
1 cup	**(*250 mL*) cooked broccoli flowerets**
½ cup	**(*125 mL*) grated Parmesan cheese**
	Hot cooked spaghetti

■ In 10-inch (*25 cm*) skillet over medium heat, in hot oil, cook chicken and onion until chicken is browned and onion is tender.

■ Stir in soup, milk and sherry. Add mushrooms, broccoli and ½ cup (*125 mL*) cheese. Reduce heat to low. Cover; cook 10 minutes or until chicken is no longer pink, stirring occasionally.

■ Serve over spaghetti. Serve with additional cheese, if desired.

TIP: If you like, next time substitute ½ cup (*125 mL*) thinly sliced green and sweet red peppers for the broccoli.

Makes 4 servings.

CHICKEN MOZZARELLA

4	**skinless, boneless chicken breast halves (about 1 lb / *450 g*)**
2 tbsp	**(*30 mL*) all-purpose flour**
1 tsp	**(*5 mL*) dried basil leaves, crushed**
1 tbsp	**(*15 mL*) oil**
1 can	**CAMPBELL'S condensed Tomato Soup**
2 tbsp	**(*30 mL*) water**
4	**slices mozzarella cheese**
¼ cup	**(*50 mL*) chopped green pepper**

■ Place chicken breasts between 2 sheets of plastic wrap. With flat side of meat mallet or rolling pin, pound chicken to ¼-inch (*0,5 cm*) thickness. On waxed paper, mix flour and basil. Coat chicken lightly with flour mixture.

■ In 10-inch (*25 cm*) skillet over medium-high heat, in hot oil, cook chicken 10 minutes or until chicken is browned on both sides.

■ Add soup and water, stirring to loosen browned bits. Reduce heat to low. Cover; cook 5 minutes or until chicken is no longer pink.

■ Uncover; top each chicken breast with a cheese slice and sprinkle with green pepper. Heat until cheese begins to melt.

Makes 4 servings.

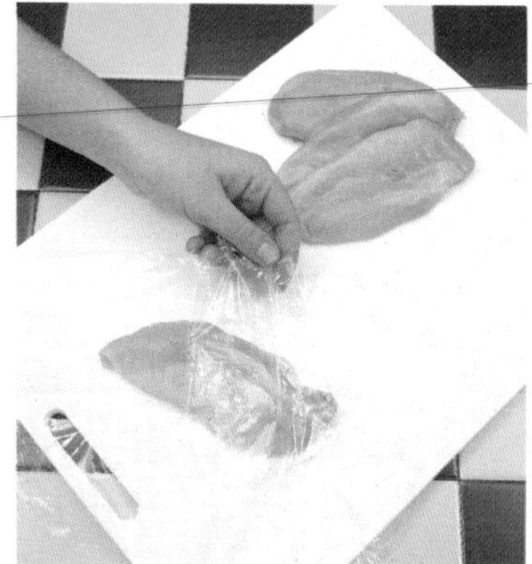

1 Place chicken between 2 sheets of plastic wrap.

2 Pound the chicken using a meat mallet.

3 Cook chicken in a skillet until browned on both sides.

4 Add soup and water to skillet. Stir to loosen browned bits.

CHICKEN MOZZARELLA

TURKEY-VEGETABLE POT PIE

1 pkg (16 oz)	**(*450 g*) frozen mixed vegetables (about 4 cups / *1 L* of broccoli, cauliflower and carrots)**
2 tbsp	**(*30 mL*) margarine *or* butter**
½ cup	**(*125 mL*) chopped onion**
½ cup	**(*125 mL*) sliced celery**
½ tsp	**(*2 mL*) dried thyme leaves, crushed**
1 can	**CAMPBELL'S condensed Cream of Broccoli *or* Cream of Mushroom Soup**
1 can	**CAMPBELL'S condensed Cream of Chicken Soup**
1 cup	**(*250 mL*) milk**
3 cups	**(*750 mL*) diced cooked turkey *or* chicken**
¼ tsp	**(*1 mL*) pepper**
1 pkg (8 oz)	**(*235 g*) refrigerated crescent rolls***

■ Preheat oven to 375 °F (*190 °C*). Cook vegetables according to package directions; drain.

■ Meanwhile, in 2-quart (*2 L*) saucepan over medium heat, in hot margarine, cook onion, celery and thyme until onion is tender, stirring occasionally. Add soups and milk; stir until smooth.

■ In 12- by 8-inch (*30 x 20 cm*) baking dish, combine turkey, cooked vegetables and pepper. Add soup mixture, stirring gently to mix.

■ Unroll crescent rolls without separating pieces. Firmly press perforations to seal. Cut dough lengthwise into 8 strips, about ¾ inch (*2 cm*) wide. Arrange dough strips over chicken mixture to form a lattice, cutting strips as necessary to fit. Press ends of strips to baking dish.

■ Bake 30 minutes or until golden brown. Cover edges with foil after 20 minutes of baking if pastry browns too quickly. Let stand 5 minutes before serving.

** If not available at your food market, substitute a pastry for one-crust pie. On lightly floured surface, roll pastry into a 14- by 9-inch (36 X 23 cm) rectangle. Cut pastry lengthwise into eight strips, each about 1 inch (2,5 cm) wide. Continue as directed above. Bake in 425°F (220°C) oven until golden brown.*

Makes 6 servings.

TURKEY-VEGETABLE POT PIE

SPANISH CHICKEN AND RICE

2 tbsp	**(*30 mL*) vegetable oil**
2½- to 3-lb	**(*1,1- to 1,4-kg*) broiler-fryer chicken, cut up**
1 can	**CAMPBELL'S condensed Chicken Broth**
1 cup	**(*250 mL*) chopped green pepper**
1 can (about 8 oz)	**(*225 mL*) tomatoes, drained and chopped**
⅔ cup	**(*150 mL*) *uncooked* regular long-grain rice**
3	**cloves garlic, minced**
2 tbsp	**(*30 mL*) chopped pimento**
¼ tsp	**(*1 mL*) hot pepper sauce**
	Fresh parsley sprigs for garnish

■ In 10-inch (*25 cm*) skillet over medium-high heat, in hot oil, cook chicken 10 minutes or until browned on all sides. Spoon off fat.

■ Stir in broth, green pepper, tomatoes, rice, garlic, pimento and hot pepper sauce. Reduce heat to low. Cover; cook 35 minutes or until liquid is absorbed and chicken is no longer pink and juices run clear.

■ To serve, spoon some rice mixture on each plate and top with chicken. Garnish with parsley, if desired.

TIP: When you shop, select chicken that is plump; that's a good indication it will be moist and meaty. Also look for poultry with skin that is white to deep yellow with no bruises or discoloration.

Makes 4 servings.

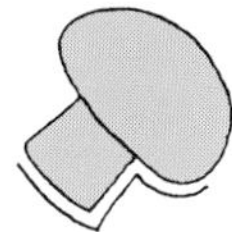

GARDEN CHICKEN AND STUFFING

¼ cup	**(*50 mL*) margarine *or* butter**
1 cup	**(*250 mL*) chopped celery**
1 cup	**(*250 mL*) chopped onion**
1 cup	**(*250 mL*) chopped carrots**
¼ cup	**(*50 mL*) all-purpose flour**
1 can	**CAMPBELL'S condensed Chicken Broth**
1 cup	**(*250 mL*) milk**
1 pkg (7 oz)	**(*200 g*) herb seasoned cubed stuffing***
2 cups	**(*500 mL*) cubed cooked chicken *or* turkey**
1 cup	**(*250 mL*) shredded Cheddar cheese**

■ In 3-quart (*3 L*) saucepan over medium heat, in hot margarine, cook celery, onion and carrots until tender. Add flour; cook 1 minute more, stirring constantly. Gradually stir in broth and milk. Cook until mixture boils and thickens, stirring constantly.

■ Add stuffing and chicken; toss to coat. Spoon into 12- by 8-inch (*30 x 20 cm*) baking dish. Bake at 350 °F (*180 °C*) for 35 minutes. Sprinkle with cheese. Bake 5 minutes more or until cheese melts. Garnish with *celery leaves* and *carrot curls*, if desired.

* **TIP**: You can substitute 4 cups (*1 L*) herb-seasoned croutons (8 ounces / *225 g*) for the stuffing cubes.

Makes 6 servings.

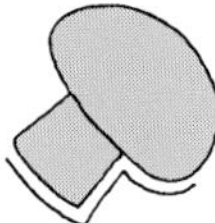

CHICKEN BROCCOLI ORIENTALE

	Broth-Simmered Rice (see recipe, page 132) *or* hot cooked rice
1 tbsp	**(*15 mL*) vegetable oil**
1 lb	**(*450 g*) skinless, boneless chicken breasts *or* thighs, cut into strips**
1	**small onion, cut into 1-inch (*2,5 cm*) pieces**
1	**medium sweet red *or* green pepper, cut into 1-inch (*2,5 cm*) squares**
1 can	**CAMPBELL'S condensed Cream of Broccoli *or* Cream of Chicken Soup**
3 tbsp	**(*45 mL*) water**
1 tbsp	**(*15 mL*) soy sauce**
	Green onion (spring onion) for garnish
	Soy sauce

■ Prepare Broth-Simmered Rice as directed. Meanwhile, in 10-inch (*25 cm*) skillet over medium-high heat, in hot oil, cook chicken *half* at a time, until browned. Remove; set aside. Repeat with remaining chicken.

■ Return chicken to skillet. Add onion and pepper. Cook 5 minutes or until vegetables are tender-crisp and chicken is no longer pink.

■ Stir in soup, water and 1 tablespoon (*15 mL*) soy sauce. Heat to boiling. Reduce heat to low. Cover; cook 5 minutes, stirring occasionally.

■ Serve chicken mixture over rice. Garnish with green onion and pass additional soy sauce, if desired.

Makes about 3½ cups (875 mL) or 4 main-dish servings.

1 Cook chicken, half at a time, until browned.

2 Return all browned chicken to skillet.

3 Add onion and pepper. Cook 5 minutes.

CHICKEN BROCCOLI ORIENTALE

4 Stir in soup, water and soy sauce. Heat mixture to boiling.

CREAMY CHICKEN LASAGNA

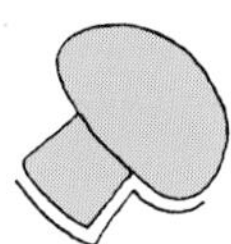

CREAMY CHICKEN LASAGNA

2 cups	**(*500 mL*) shredded mozzarella cheese (8 oz / *225 g*), divided**
2 cans	**CAMPBELL'S condensed Cream of Mushroom Soup**
1½ cups	**(*375 mL*) milk**
⅛ tsp	**(*0,5 mL*) ground nutmeg**
⅛ tsp	**(*0,5 mL*) ground red pepper (cayenne)**
1 pkg (10 oz)	**(*285 g*) frozen chopped spinach, thawed and *well drained***
1	**egg**
1 container (15 oz)	**(*425 g*) ricotta cheese**
12	**lasagna noodles, cooked and drained**
2 cups	**(*500 mL*) diced cooked chicken**
½ cup	**(*125 mL*) grated Parmesan cheese**

■ Reserve ⅔ *cup (150 mL)* of mozzarella cheese for top layer. In medium bowl, combine soup, milk, nutmeg and red pepper; set aside.

■ In another medium bowl, combine spinach, egg and ricotta; mix well.

■ In bottom of 13- by 9-inch *(33 x 23 cm)* baking dish, spread ½ cup *(125 mL)* of soup mixture. Arrange 4 lasagna noodles on mixture. Top with ⅓ of remaining soup mixture, ½ of spinach mixture, ½ of remaining mozzarella and ½ of the chicken. Repeat layers ending with remaining noodles, soup mixture, reserved ⅔ cup *(150 mL)* mozzarella cheese and Parmesan cheese.

■ Bake at 350 °F *(180°C)* for 40 minutes or until hot and bubbling. Let stand 15 minutes before serving.

Makes 8 servings.

CHICKEN ENCHILADAS

1 can	**CAMPBELL'S condensed Cream of Chicken *or* Cream of Celery Soup**
½ cup	**(*125 mL*) sour cream**
2 tbsp	**(*30 mL*) margarine *or* butter**
½ cup	**(*125 mL*) chopped onion**
1 tsp	**(*5 mL*) chili powder**
2 cups	**(*500 mL*) diced cooked chicken**
1 can (4 oz)	**(*110 g*) chopped green chilies**
8	**flour tortillas (7-inch / *17,5 cm*)**
1 cup	**(*250 mL*) shredded Monterey Jack or Cheddar cheese (4 oz / *120 g*)**
	Fresh parsley for garnish

■ Preheat oven to 375 °F (*190 °C*). In small bowl, stir together soup and sour cream until smooth; set aside.

■ In 2-quart (*2 L*) saucepan over medium heat, in hot margarine, cook onion and chili powder until onion is tender, stirring often. Stir in chicken, chilies and 2 tablespoons (*30 mL*) of soup mixture. Remove from heat.

■ *To make enchiladas:* Along center of each tortilla, spread about ¼ cup (*50 mL*) of chicken mixture; fold sides over filling and place seam-side down in greased 12- by 8- inch (*30 x 20 cm*) baking dish.

■ Spread remaining soup mixture over enchiladas. Cover with foil; bake 15 minutes. Sprinkle with cheese. Bake, uncovered, 5 minutes more or until cheese melts. Garnish with parsley, if desired.

Makes 4 servings.

1 Cook onion and chili powder over medium heat.

2 Add the chicken pieces, chilies and 2 tbsp (*30 mL*) of soup mixture.

CHICKEN ENCHILADAS

3 Spread ¼ cup (*50 mL*) of chicken mixture along center of each tortilla.

4 Fold sides over filling and arrange seam-side down in greased baking dish.

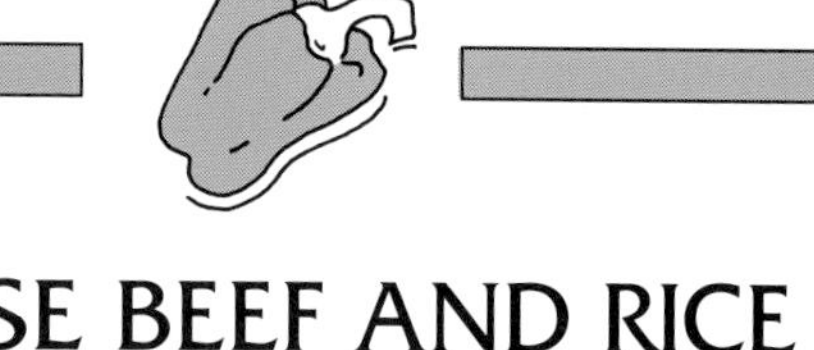

ANISE BEEF AND RICE

- **2 tbsp** **(*30 mL*) vegetable oil**
- **1 lb** **(*450 g*) boneless beef top round steak, thinly sliced**
- **3 cups** **(*750 mL*) coarsely chopped bok choy *or* Chinese cabbage**
- **½ cup** **(*125 mL*) yellow squash *or* zucchini cut in 2-inch (*5 cm*) matchstick-thin strips**
- **1 can** **CAMPBELL'S condensed Beef Broth ***
- **¼ cup** **(*50 mL*) dry sherry**
- **2 tbsp** **(*30 mL*) soy sauce**
- **¼ tsp** **(*1 mL*) anise seed**
- **2 tbsp** **(*30 mL*) cornstarch (cornflour)**
- **½ cup** **(*125 mL*) water**
- **1 cup** **(*250 mL*) halved cherry tomatoes**

■ In 10-inch (*25 cm*) skillet over high heat, in hot oil, cook beef, *half* at a time, until beef just changes color, stirring constantly. Transfer to bowl.

■ Add bok choy and squash to skillet. Over high heat, cook 1 minute, stirring often. Stir in broth, sherry, soy and anise. Heat to boiling.

■ Meanwhile, in bowl, stir together cornstarch and water until smooth; gradually stir into broth mixture. Cook until mixture boils and thickens, stirring often. Add cooked beef and cherry tomatoes. Cook 2 minutes or until heated through, stirring often. Serve over hot cooked *rice*.

** CAMPBELL'S condensed Consommé (Beef) in the U.K.*

Makes about 5 cups (1,3 L) or 4 servings.

GERMAN-STYLE POT ROAST

1 tbsp	**(*15 mL*) vegetable oil**
3- to 3½-lb	**(*1,3- to 1,6-kg*) boneless beef chuck eye roast**
1 can	**CAMPBELL'S condensed French Onion Soup** *
1 soup can	**water**
½ cup	**(*125 mL*) vinegar**
2	**medium bay leaves**
¼ tsp	**(*1 mL*) pepper**
⅛ tsp	**(*0,5 mL*) ground cloves**
6	**small potatoes, cut into chunks**
3	**medium carrots, cut into chunks**
3	**medium parsnips, peeled and cut into ¼-inch (*0,5 cm*) strips**
¼ cup	**(*50 mL*) finely crushed gingersnaps**

* *Not available in the U.K.*

■ In 6-quart (*6 L*) Dutch oven over medium-high heat, in hot oil, brown roast on all sides. Spoon off fat.

■ Stir in soup, water, vinegar, bay leaves, pepper and cloves. Reduce heat to low. Cover; cook 1½ hours. Add potatoes and carrots. Cover; cook 30 minutes.

■ Add parsnips. Cover; cook 30 minutes or until roast and vegetables are fork-tender.

■ Remove roast and vegetables to serving platter. Remove bay leaves. Skim off fat from liquid in Dutch oven. Stir in gingersnaps. Cook until thickened, stirring occasionally. Serve gravy over roast and vegetables. Garnish with fresh *parsley sprigs*, if desired.

Makes 8 servings.

LONDON BROIL WITH MUSHROOM SAUCE

1½ lb	**(*675 g*) beef top round steak (about 1½ inches / *3,5 cm* thick)**
2 tbsp	**(*30 mL*) margarine *or* butter**
2 cups	**(*500 mL*) sliced fresh mushrooms**
½ cup	**(*125 mL*) sliced onion**
1 can	**CAMPBELL'S condensed Cream of Mushroom Soup**
¼ cup	**(*50 mL*) water**
2 tsp	**(*10 mL*) Worcestershire sauce**
	Fluted fresh mushrooms, celery leaves and orange peel for garnish

■ On unheated rack of broiler pan, place steak. Position broiler pan in oven so top of meat is 4 inches (*10 cm*) from heat. Broil 15 minutes for rare or until desired doneness, turning meat halfway through cooking.

■ Meanwhile, in 10-inch (*25 cm*) skillet over medium-high heat, in hot margarine, cook mushrooms and onion 10 minutes or until liquid evaporates and onion is browned. Stir in soup, water and Worcestershire sauce. Heat through, stirring occasionally.

■ Thinly slice meat diagonally across the grain. Spoon some sauce over meat; pass remaining sauce. Garnish with mushrooms, celery leaves and orange peel, if desired.

TIP: Believe it or not, London Broil is an American dish. It is a beefsteak, often a flank steak, that's broiled and cut across the grain into thin slices. Usually served with a savory sauce, this classic steak can be made with other cuts of meat, such as a top round.

Makes about 1½ cups (375 mL) sauce and 6 main-dish servings.

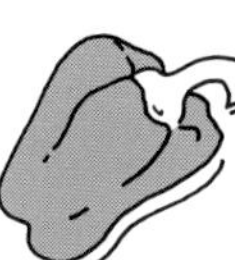

LONDON BROIL WITH MUSHROOM SAUCE

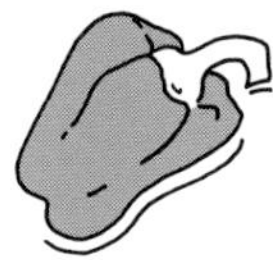

Northern-Style Lasagna

4	**slices bacon, diced**
1 lb	**(*450 g*) ground beef**
1 cup	**(*250 mL*) chopped onion**
3 cups	**(*750 mL*) spaghetti sauce**
1 can	**CAMPBELL'S condensed Cream of Mushroom Soup**
½ soup can	**milk**
1 container (15 oz)	**(*425 g*) ricotta cheese**
½ cup	**(*125 mL*) grated Parmesan cheese (2 oz / *60 g*), divided**
9	**lasagna noodles, cooked and drained**

■ In 10-inch (*25 cm*) skillet over medium-high heat, cook bacon until crisp. Spoon off fat.

■ Add beef and onion. Cook until meat is browned and is thoroughly cooked and no pink remains, stirring once during cooking to separate meat. Spoon off fat. Stir in spaghetti sauce, set aside.

■ Meanwhile, in small bowl, combine soup and milk. In another small bowl, combine ricotta and *¼ cup (50 mL)* of Parmesan.

■ In 13- by 9-inch (*33 x 23 cm*) baking dish, spread *1½ cups (375 mL)* of meat sauce. Top with 3 lasagna noodles, spread with ½ of soup mixture, ½ of cheese mixture, and ⅓ of remaining meat sauce. Repeat layers. Top with remaining lasagna noodles and remaining meat sauce. Cover with foil.

■ Bake at 375 °F (*190 °C*) for 30 minutes. Uncover, sprinkle with remaining ¼ cup (*50 mL*) Parmesan. Bake 10 minutes more or until hot and bubbling. Let stand 10 minutes before serving.

TIP: In northern Italy many lasagna recipes often use a creamy white sauce along with the traditional red sauce.

Makes 8 servings.

1 Add beef and onion; cook thoroughly.

NORTHERN-STYLE LASAGNA

2 Combine soup and milk in a small bowl, and ricotta and Parmesan in another bowl.

3 Place lasagna noodles over meat sauce in baking dish.

4 Spread half of soup mixture over noodles.

HAMBURGER 'N' FIXINGS SANDWICHES

1 lb	**(*450 g*) ground beef**
2 loaves	**French bread (*each* 14 inches /*35 cm* long), split lengthwise***
1 can	**CAMPBELL'S condensed French Onion Soup ****
¼ cup	**(*50 mL*) ketchup**
2 tbsp	**(*30 mL*) finely chopped sweet pickle**
2 tsp	**(*10 mL*) spicy brown mustard *or* French mustard**
⅛ tsp	**(*0,5 mL*) pepper**
	Desired toppings

*** Not available in the U.K.*

■ In 10-inch (*25 cm*) skillet over medium heat, cook beef until browned, stirring to separate meat. Spoon off fat. Meanwhile, toast French bread.

■ Stir soup, ketchup, pickle, mustard and pepper into skillet. Heat to boiling. Reduce heat to low; heat through. Divide *half* of beef mixture between each loaf. Top with desired toppings. To serve, cut each loaf in half.

TIP: Serve an assortment of toppers with this sandwich: chopped onion, leaf lettuce, pickle relish and sliced tomatoes.

** For 4 individual sandwiches, use 4 hard rolls (each 8 inches / 20 cm long), split lengthwise.*

Makes 4 main-dish servings.

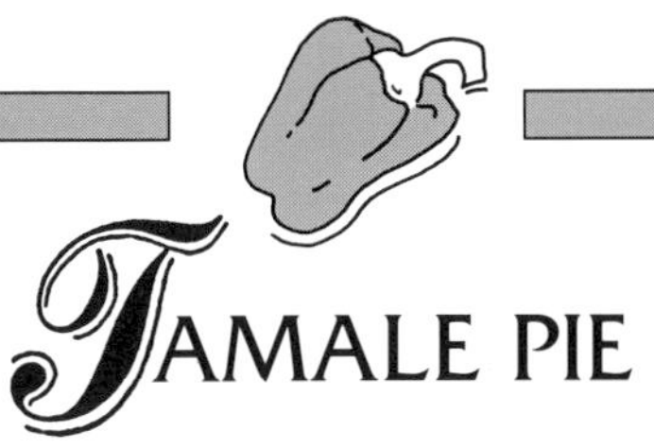

TAMALE PIE

1 lb	**(*450 g*) ground beef**
2 tsp	**(*10 mL*) chili powder**
1 can	**CAMPBELL'S condensed Tomato Soup**
1 cup	**(*250 mL*) chopped green pepper**
1 cup	**(*250 mL*) whole kernel corn (sweet corn)**
½ cup	**(*125 mL*) salsa *or* taco sauce**
¼ cup	**(*50 mL*) water**
1 pkg (8½ to 12 oz)	**(*240 to 340 g*) corn muffin mix**

■ Preheat oven to 400 °F (*200 °C*). In 10-inch (*25 cm*) skillet over medium heat, cook beef and chili powder until beef is browned, stirring to separate meat. Spoon off fat.

■ Stir in soup, pepper, corn, salsa and water. Heat to boiling. Reduce heat to low. Cover; cook 5 minutes. Pour into 2-quart (*2 L*) casserole. Prepare corn muffin mix according to package directions; spoon evenly over soup mixture.

■ Bake 25 minutes or until a wooden toothpick inserted in center of muffin mixture comes out clean.

Makes 6 servings.

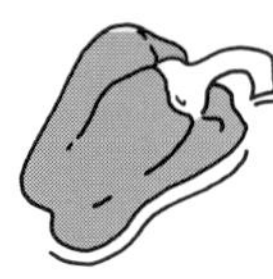

FOOLPROOF BEEF AND BROCCOLI

¾ lb	**(*350 g*) boneless beef sirloin steak (about ¾-inch / *2 cm* thick)**
1 tbsp	**(*15 mL*) vegetable oil**
1	**clove garlic, minced**
2 cups	**(*500 mL*) broccoli flowerets**
1	**medium onion, cut into wedges**
1 can	**CAMPBELL'S condensed Cream of Broccoli *or* Cream of Mushroom Soup**
¼ cup	**(*50 mL*) water**
1 tbsp	**(*15 mL*) soy sauce**
	Hot cooked noodles
	Cherry tomatoes for garnish

■ Slice beef across the grain into thin strips.

■ In 10-inch (*25 cm*) skillet over medium-high heat, in hot oil, cook beef and garlic, *half* at a time, until beef is browned. Return beef to skillet. Add broccoli and onion. Cook 5 minutes, stirring often.

■ Stir in soup, water and soy sauce. Heat to boiling. Reduce heat to low. Cover; cook 5 minutes or until vegetables are tender. Serve over noodles. Garnish with cherry tomatoes, if desired.

TIP: To make slicing the meat easier, freeze beef about 1 hour before cutting into thin strips.

Makes 4 servings.

FOOLPROOF BEEF AND BROCCOLI

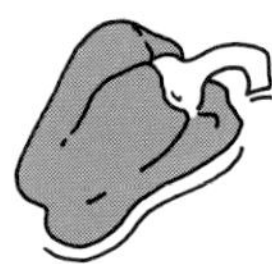

SPICY BROCCOLI BEEF

1 can	**CAMPBELL'S condensed Beef Broth** *
½ cup	**(*125 mL*) water**
2 tbsp	**(*30 mL*) cornstarch (cornflour)**
1 tbsp	**(*15 mL*) soy sauce**
½ tsp	**(*2 mL*) crushed red pepper**
2 tbsp	**(*30 mL*) peanut oil**
4 cups	**(*1 L*) broccoli flowerets**
2	**green onions (spring onions), diagonally sliced**
1 lb	**(*450 g*) boneless beef sirloin steak, thinly sliced**

** CAMPBELL'S condensed Consommé (Beef) in the U.K.*

■ In bowl, combine broth, water, cornstarch, soy sauce and red pepper; set aside.

■ In 10-inch *(25 cm)* skillet over high heat, in *1 tablespoon (15 mL)* hot oil, stir-fry broccoli and onions 2 minutes or until tender-crisp. Transfer to bowl.

■ In same skillet over high heat, in remaining hot oil, stir-fry beef, *half* at a time, until color just changes. Transfer to bowl with broccoli.

■ Stir broth mixture into skillet. Cook over high heat until mixture boils and thickens, stirring often. Add broccoli-beef mixture; heat through. Serve over hot cooked *noodles.* Serve with additional *soy sauce,* if desired.

Makes about 4 cups (1 L) or 4 servings.

1 Combine broth, water, cornstarch, soy and red pepper.

2 Stir-fry broccoli and green onions.

3 Stir broth mixture into skillet and cook until thickened.

SPICY BROCCOLI BEEF

PIQUANT PORK CHOPS

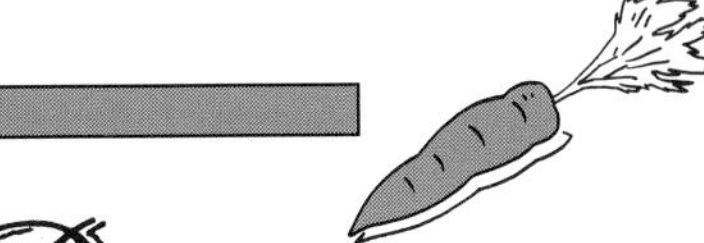

PIQUANT PORK CHOPS

4	**boneless pork chops, each cut ¾ inch (*2 cm*) thick (about 1 lb /*450 g*)**
¼ tsp	**(*1 mL*) pepper**
1 tbsp	**(*15 mL*) vegetable oil**
1 can	**CAMPBELL'S condensed Chicken Broth**
3 tbsp	**(*45 mL*) lime juice**
1 tbsp	**(*15 mL*) sugar**
1 tsp	**(*5 mL*) Dijon-style mustard**
4 tsp	**(*20 mL*) cornstarch (cornflour)**
2 tbsp	**(*30 mL*) water**
	Desired hot cooked rice
	Fresh lime slice *and* parsley for garnish

■ Sprinkle chops with pepper. In 10-inch (*25 cm*) skillet over medium heat, in hot oil, cook chops 10 minutes or until browned on both sides. Spoon off fat.

■ Stir in broth, lime juice, sugar and mustard. Heat to boiling. Reduce heat to low. Cover; cook 10 minutes until chops are fork-tender, stirring occasionally.

■ Transfer chops to platter. In bowl, stir together cornstarch and water until smooth; gradually stir into skillet. Over high heat, cook until mixture boils and thickens, stirring constantly. Serve with rice. Garnish with lime slice and parsley, if desired.

TIP: Accompany with a fresh fruit salad sprinkled with a little lemon or lime juice.

Makes 4 servings.

GARDEN PORK SAUTÉ

2 tbsp	**(*30 mL*) margarine *or* butter, divided**
4	**boneless pork chops, each cut ¾ inch (*2 cm*) thick *or* 1 lb (*450 g*) pork tenderloin, cut into ½- inch (*1 cm*) thick slices**
1 cup	**(*250 mL*) broccoli flowerets**
1 cup	**(*250 mL*) sliced fresh mushrooms**
½ cup	**(*125 mL*) diagonally sliced carrot**
1 can	**CAMPBELL'S condensed Cream of Broccoli *or* Cream of Chicken Soup**
⅓ cup	**(*75 mL*) milk**
3	**slices bacon, cooked and crumbled**
⅛ tsp	**(*0,5 mL*) pepper**
	Hot cooked noodles, optional

■ In 10-inch (*25 cm*) skillet over medium-high heat, in *1 tablespoon* (*15 mL*) of hot margarine, cook pork 10 minutes or until browned on both sides. Remove pork; keep warm.

■ In same skillet, in remaining 1 tablespoon (*15 mL*) margarine, cook broccoli, mushrooms and carrot 5 minutes, stirring often. Stir in soup, milk, bacon and pepper. Heat to boiling.

■ Return pork to skillet. Reduce heat to low. Cover; cook 5 minutes or until pork is fork-tender. Serve with noodles, if desired.

Makes 4 servings.

1 Cook pork 10 minutes in skillet.

2 Remove pork and keep warm.

GARDEN PORK SAUTÉ

3 Add vegetables to skillet.

4 Stir in soup, milk, bacon and pepper.

TORTELLINI WITH MUSHROOMS AND HAM

1 tbsp	**(*15 mL*) olive oil**
½ cup	**(*125 mL*) cooked ham, cut into strips**
¼ cup	**(*50 mL*) chopped onion**
1	**clove garlic, minced**
½ tsp	**(*2 mL*) dried basil leaves, crushed**
1 can	**CAMPBELL'S condensed Cream of Mushroom Soup**
1 cup	**(*250 mL*) frozen peas**
1 soup can	**milk**
2 tbsp	**(*30 mL*) chopped fresh parsley**
⅛ tsp	**(*0,5 mL*) black pepper**
3 cups	**(*750 mL*) hot cooked cheese-filled tortellini (2 cups /*500 mL* uncooked)***
	Grated Parmesan cheese
	Sweet red pepper strips for garnish

■ In 2-quart (*2 L*) saucepan over medium heat, in hot oil, cook ham, onion, garlic and basil 2 minutes, stirring often.

■ Stir in soup and peas; heat to boiling. Reduce heat to low. Cover; cook 5 minutes or until peas are tender.

■ Stir in milk, parsley and pepper; heat through. In large bowl, pour soup mixture over tortellini; toss lightly to coat. Serve with cheese. Garnish with red pepper strips, if desired.

**If not available at your food market, substitute 3 cups (750 mL) cooked and drained corkscrew macaroni.*

Makes 4 cups (1 L) or 4 servings.

TORTELLINI WITH MUSHROOMS AND HAM

SAUSAGE STUFFING BROCCOLI BAKE

1 pkg (10 oz)	**(*285 g*) frozen chopped broccoli (*2 cups / 500 mL*)**
½ lb	**(*225 g*) bulk pork sausage**
3 cups	**(*750 mL*) plain croutons**
2 cups	**(*500 mL*) shredded sharp Cheddar, Swiss *or* Emmental cheese**
1 can	**CAMPBELL'S condensed Cream of Broccoli *or* Cream of Chicken Soup**
4	**eggs**
1 soup can	**milk**

■ Preheat oven to 400 °F (*200 °C*). Cook broccoli according to package directions; drain.

■ Meanwhile, in 10-inch (*25 cm*) skillet over medium heat, cook sausage until browned and no longer pink, stirring to separate meat. Spoon off fat.

■ In large bowl, combine cooked sausage, cooked broccoli, croutons and cheese. Arrange mixture evenly in greased 12- by 8-inch (*30 x 20 cm*) baking dish.

■ In same bowl, stir soup until smooth. Beat in eggs and milk. Pour over sausage mixture, covering all ingredients. Bake 30 minutes or until set in center. Let stand 10 minutes before serving. Cut into squares to serve.

Makes 9 servings.

PORK NORMANDY

1 tbsp	**(*15 mL*) vegetable oil**
6	**pork chops, each cut ½-inch (*1 cm*) thick (about 1½ lb / *675 g*)**
1 can	**CAMPBELL'S condensed Cream of Mushroom Soup**
½ cup	**(*125 mL*) apple juice**
1	**medium apple, chopped**
½ cup	**(*125 mL*) sliced celery**
¼ tsp	**(*1 mL*) dried thyme leaves, crushed**
	Hot cooked noodles
	Apple slices *and* thyme sprig for garnish

■ In 10-inch (*25 cm*) skillet over medium heat, in hot oil, cook chops, *half* at a time, about 10 minutes or until browned on both sides. Spoon off fat. Remove chops.

■ Add soup, apple juice, chopped apple, celery and thyme to skillet; stir. Heat to boiling. Return chops to skillet. Reduce heat to low. Cover; cook 10 minutes or until pork is fork-tender, stirring occasionally.

■ Serve over hot cooked noodles. Garnish with apple slices and thyme sprig, if desired.

Makes 6 servings.

PLUM GLAZED HAM

PLUM GLAZED HAM

5- to 7-lb	**(*2,2- to 3-kg*) fully cooked smoked rump *or* shank half ham**
3 tbsp	**(*45 mL*) cornstarch (cornflour)**
1 can	**CAMPBELL'S condensed Beef Broth** *
1 can (16 oz)	**(*450 mL*) purple plums, drained, pitted and puréed****
½ cup	**(*125 mL*) orange marmalade**
2 tbsp	**(*30 mL*) prepared mustard *or* mild English mustard**
	Plum halves *and* orange slices for garnish

** CAMPBELL'S condensed Consommé (Beef) in the U.K.*

■ On rack in roasting pan, place ham fat-side up. With sharp knife, score fat into ¾-inch (*2 cm*) squares. Insert meat thermometer into thickest part of meat, not touching bone or fat. Bake at 325 °F (*160 °C*) for 45 minutes.

■ Meanwhile, in 2-quart (*2 L*) saucepan, stir together cornstarch and broth until smooth. Stir in plum purée, marmalade and mustard. Over high heat, heat to boiling, stirring often. Reduce heat to medium; cook 5 minutes, stirring occasionally until sauce is slightly thickened. Use *¾ cup (175 mL)* of sauce to glaze ham; set remaining sauce aside.

■ Bake ham 1 hour or until thermometer reads 140 °F (*60 °C*), basting occasionally with sauce. Let stand 10 minutes before carving. Heat remaining sauce. Serve with ham. Garnish with additional plums and orange slices, if desired.

*** If not available at your food market, substitute 1 can (16 ounces / 450 mL) sliced peaches, drained and puréed, for the plums and use only 2 tablespoons (30 mL) cornstarch (cornflour).*

Makes 10 to 14 servings.

HERBED PORK CHOPS

2 tbsp	**(*30 mL*) all-purpose flour**
¼ tsp	**(*1 mL*) ground sage**
¼ tsp	**(*1 mL*) dried thyme leaves, crushed**
4	**boneless pork chops, each cut ¾ inch (*2 cm*) thick (about 1 lb / *450 g*)**
2 tbsp	**(*30 mL*) margarine *or* butter**
1 can	**CAMPBELL'S condensed Cream of Chicken Soup**
½ cup	**(*125 mL*) water**
	Hot cooked rice *or* prepared long-grain and wild rice mix
	Fresh thyme sprigs, orange slices *and* radicchio leaves for garnish

■ On waxed paper, combine flour, sage and thyme. Coat chops lightly with flour mixture.

■ In 10-inch (*25 cm*) skillet over medium-high heat, in hot margarine, cook chops 10 minutes or until browned on both sides. Push chops to one side of skillet.

■ Stir in soup and water, stirring to loosen browned bits. Reduce heat to low. Cover; cook 5 minutes or until chops are fork-tender. Serve chops with rice; spoon sauce over. Garnish with thyme, orange slices and radicchio, if desired.

Makes 4 servings.

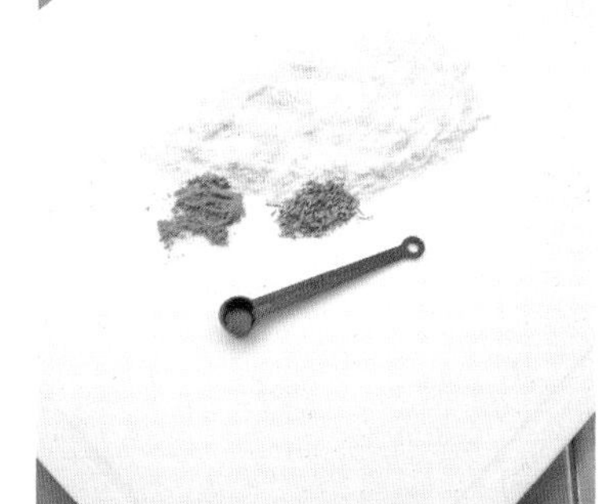

1 Combine flour, sage and thyme.

2 Coat chops lightly with flour mixture.

3 Cook chops in hot margarine.

4 Stir in soup and water.

HERBED PORK CHOPS

TOMATO-BASIL PORK CHOPS

1 tbsp	**(*15 mL*) olive oil**
6	**boneless pork chops, each cut ¾ inch (*2 cm*) thick (about 1½ lb / *675 g*)**
1 can	**CAMPBELL'S condensed Tomato Soup**
1	**medium onion, finely chopped**
½ tsp	**(*2 mL*) dried basil leaves, crushed**
⅛ tsp	**(*0,5 mL*) black pepper**
2 tbsp	**(*30 mL*) water**
1	**orange, sliced**
1	**green pepper, cut into strips**
	Desired hot cooked rice

■ In 10-inch (*25 cm*) skillet over medium heat, in hot oil, cook chops, *half* at a time, about 10 minutes or until browned on both sides. Spoon off fat.

■ Add soup, onion, basil, pepper and water to skillet; stir until smooth. Add orange and green pepper. Heat to boiling. Return chops to skillet. Reduce heat to low. Cover; cook 10 minutes or until chops are fork-tender, stirring occasionally. Serve over rice.

Makes 6 servings.

BAVARIAN KIELBASA WITH NOODLES

6 oz	**(*180 g*) *uncooked* egg noodles**
¾ lb	**(*350 g*) smoked kielbasa *or* cooked ham, cut up**
1	**large onion, sliced**
1 can	**CAMPBELL'S condensed Cream of Mushroom Soup**
1 soup can	**milk**
1½ cups	**(*375 mL*) frozen cut green beans**
¼ tsp	**(*1 mL*) pepper**
	Spicy brown mustard *or* French mustard

■ Cook noodles according to package directions; drain. Meanwhile, in 10-inch (*25 cm*) skillet over medium heat, cook kielbasa and onion until browned, stirring often. Spoon off fat.

■ Add soup; stir until smooth. Gradually stir in milk. Add beans and pepper. Heat to boiling. Reduce heat to low. Cover; cook 5 minutes or until beans are tender, stirring occasionally.

■ Stir cooked noodles into skillet. Heat 2 minutes, stirring often. Serve with mustard, if desired.

Makes 6 cups (1,5 L) or 4 servings.

LAMB CURRY

2 tbsp	**(*30 mL*) vegetable oil**
1½ lb	**(*675 g*) lean lamb cubes**
2 tsp	**(*10 mL*) curry powder**
1	**clove garlic, minced**
1 tsp	**(*5 mL*) grated fresh ginger**
⅛ tsp	**(*0,5 mL*) ground cumin**
1 can	**CAMPBELL'S condensed French Onion Soup ***
1 soup can	**water**
1 can (8 oz)	**(*225 mL*) *undrained* stewed tomatoes**
2 cups	**(*500 mL*) cubed peeled potatoes**
	Lemon slices for garnish

** Not available in the U.K.*

■ In 10-inch (*25 cm*) skillet over medium heat, in hot oil, cook lamb, a few pieces at a time, until browned on all sides. Transfer to paper towels to drain.

■ Reduce heat to low. To hot drippings, stir in curry powder, garlic, ginger and cumin. Return lamb to skillet; stir to coat with curry mixture.

■ Stir in soup, water and tomatoes. Cover; cook 45 minutes, stirring occasionally.

■ Add potatoes; toss gently to coat. Cover; cook 20 minutes more or until potatoes are tender.

■ Garnish with lemon slices.

Makes about 5 cups (1,3 L) or 5 servings.

LAMB CURRY

RAGOUT OF VEAL AND MUSHROOMS MARSALA

1½ lb	**(*675 g*) veal cubes for stew, cut into 1½-inch (*4 cm*) pieces**
2 tbsp	**(*30 mL*) olive oil, divided**
2 tbsp	**(*30 mL*) margarine *or* butter, divided**
1	**large onion, quartered lengthwise and thinly sliced**
½ lb	**(*225 g*) mushrooms, sliced (optional)**
½ tsp	**(*2 mL*) dried thyme leaves, crushed**
⅔ cup	**(*150 mL*) Marsala**
1 can	**CAMPBELL'S condensed Cream of Mushroom Soup**
½ soup can	**water**
1 tbsp	**(*15 mL*) paprika**
½ tsp	**(*2 mL*) pepper**
	Hot cooked rice

■ Trim excess fat from veal. With flat side of meat mallet or rolling pin, pound meat to flatten slightly.

■ In 10-inch (*25 cm*) skillet over high heat, in *1 tablespoon* (*15 mL*) *each* hot oil and margarine, cook veal, *half* at a time, until browned on all sides. Set aside.

■ To hot drippings add remaining oil and margarine. Over medium heat, cook onion, mushrooms and thyme until tender, stirring occasionally. Add Marsala.

■ Stir in soup, water, paprika and pepper. Return veal and any accumulated juices to skillet. Reduce heat to low. Cover; simmer 1 hour, stirring occasionally.

■ Uncover, simmer about 20 minutes more or until veal is fork-tender and sauce is desired consistency. Serve with rice.

Makes 4 servings.

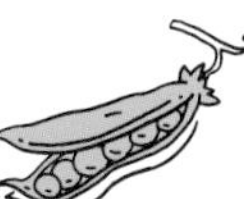

RAGOUT OF VEAL AND MUSHROOMS MARSALA

SALSA SWORDFISH

1 can	**CAMPBELL'S condensed Tomato Soup**
½ cup	**(*125 mL*) salsa *or* taco sauce**
2 tsp	**(*10 mL*) chopped fresh cilantro *or* 1 tbsp (*15 mL*) chopped fresh parsley**
2 tsp	**(*10 mL*) lime juice**
4	**swordfish steaks, each cut ¾ to 1 inch (*2* to *2,5 cm*) thick (about 2 lb / *900 g*)**
	Fresh parsley *or* cilantro *and* lime slice for garnish

■ In 10-inch (*25 cm*) skillet, combine soup, salsa, cilantro and lime juice. Over high heat, heat to boiling. Arrange steaks in soup mixture. Return to boiling. Reduce heat to low. Cover; cook 15 minutes or until fish flakes easily when tested with fork.

■ Transfer fish to platter to keep warm. Over medium heat, cook sauce until slightly thickened, stirring occasionally. Serve sauce over fish. Garnish with parsley and lime slices, if desired.

TIP: Serve steamed fresh asparagus spears for a quick and colorful accompaniment.

Makes 4 servings.

SHRIMP IN PASTRY PUFFS

6	**frozen patty shells *or* 3 cups (*750 mL*) hot cooked rice**
2 tbsp	**(*30 mL*) margarine *or* butter**
2 cups	**(*500 mL*) sliced fresh mushrooms**
1 can	**CAMPBELL'S condensed Cream of Celery Soup**
¼ cup	**(*50 mL*) Chablis *or* other dry white wine**
½ cup	**(*125 mL*) frozen peas**
1½ lb	**(*675 g*) small shrimp, shelled and deveined**

■ Preheat oven and bake patty shells according to package directions; keep warm.

■ Meanwhile, in 10-inch (*25 cm*) skillet over medium heat, in hot margarine, cook mushrooms until tender and liquid is evaporated, stirring occasionally.

■ Stir in soup, wine and peas. Heat to boiling. Stir in shrimp; cook until shrimp turn pink and opaque. Spoon shrimp mixture over patty shells. Garnish with *celery leaves*, if desired.

Makes 6 servings.

CREAMY DILL SALMON STEAKS

1 tbsp	**(*15 mL*) margarine *or* butter**
½ cup	**(*125 mL*) chopped green onions (spring onions)**
1 can	**CAMPBELL'S condensed Cream of Celery *or* Cream of Chicken Soup**
½ cup	**(*125 mL*) half-and-half *or* cream**
2 tbsp	**(*30 mL*) Chablis *or* other dry white wine**
2 tbsp	**(*30 mL*) chopped fresh dill *or* 1 tsp (*5 mL*) dried dill weed, crushed**
4	**salmon steaks, each cut 1 inch (*2,5 cm*) thick (about 2 lb / *900 g*)**
	Fresh dill for garnish

■ In 10-inch (*25 cm*) skillet over medium heat, in hot margarine, cook green onions until tender, stirring often. Add soup, half-and-half, wine and dill; stir until smooth.

■ Arrange fish steaks in soup mixture. Heat to boiling. Reduce heat to low. Cover; cook 15 minutes or until fish flakes easily when tested with fork. Serve fish with sauce. Garnish with fresh dill, if desired.

To microwave: In 12- by 8-inch (*30 x 20 cm*) microwave-safe baking dish, combine margarine and onions. Cover with vented plastic wrap; microwave on HIGH 2 minutes or until onions are tender, stirring once during cooking. Add soup, half-and-half, wine and dill; stir until smooth. Arrange fish steaks in dish with thicker portions of fish toward outside of dish. Cover; microwave on HIGH 10 to 11 minutes or until fish flakes easily when tested with fork, rotating dish twice during cooking. Let stand, covered, 5 minutes before serving.

TIP: Purchase a seasoned wild rice combo to serve with this fish—many cook in just 10 minutes.

Makes 4 servings.

CREAMY DILL SALMON STEAKS

EASY PAELLA

1 can (6½ oz)	**(*185 g*) chopped clams**
2 tbsp	**(*30 mL*) vegetable oil**
8	**chicken thighs (about 2½ lb / *1 kg*)**
1	**large onion, chopped**
1½ cups	**(*375 mL*) *uncooked* regular long-grain rice**
2	**cloves garlic, minced**
2 cans	**CAMPBELL'S condensed Chicken Broth**
½ tsp	**(*2 mL*) ground turmeric**
½ tsp	**(*2 mL*) pepper**
1 pkg (10 oz)	**(*285 g*) frozen peas**
½ lb	**(*225 g*) medium shrimp, shelled and deveined**
	Lemon wedges
	Fresh parsley for garnish

■ Drain clams, reserving liquid. Add enough water to clam liquid to make *1¼ cups (300 mL)*; set aside.

■ In 6-quart (*6 L*) Dutch oven over medium-high heat, in hot oil, cook chicken 10 minutes or until browned on all sides. Remove chicken; set aside.

■ Reduce heat to medium. In hot drippings, cook onion, rice and garlic until rice is lightly browned, stirring often. Add reserved clam liquid, broth, turmeric, pepper and chicken. Heat to boiling. Reduce heat to low. Cover; cook 30 minutes or until chicken is no longer pink and juices run clear.

■ Stir in clams, peas and shrimp. Cover; cook 5 minutes or until shrimp turn pink and opaque. Serve with lemon. Garnish with parsley, if desired.

Makes 8 servings.

1 Remove browned chicken pieces from Dutch oven.

2 Add onion, rice and garlic to hot drippings. Cook until rice is lightly browned.

EASY PAELLA

3 Add clam liquid, broth, seasonings and chicken. Heat to boiling.

4 Stir in clams, peas and shrimp. Cover and cook 5 minutes.

COD STEAKS ORIENTAL

½ lb	**(*225 g*) bok choy *or* Chinese cabbage**
2 tbsp	**(*30 mL*) cornstarch (cornflour)**
2 tbsp	**(*30 mL*) teriyaki sauce**
2 tbsp	**(*30 mL*) dry sherry**
1 can	**CAMPBELL'S condensed Chicken Broth**
4	**green onions (spring onions), cut into 2-inch (*5 cm*) diagonal pieces**
1 cup	**(*250 mL*) sweet red pepper cut in 1-inch (*2,5 cm*) strips**
⅛ tsp	**(*0,5 mL*) crushed red pepper**
4	**cod *or* halibut steaks, each cut about ¾ inch (*2 cm*) thick (about 2 lb / *900 g*)**

■ Cut bok choy stems into ¼-inch (*0,5 cm*) slices; coarsely shred leaves. In bowl, stir together cornstarch, teriyaki sauce and sherry until well blended. Set aside.

■ In 10-inch (*25 cm*) skillet over high heat, combine broth, green onions, pepper strips, crushed pepper and bok choy stems. Heat to boiling. Arrange fish over vegetable mixture. Reduce heat to low. Cover; cook 8 to 12 minutes or until fish flakes easily when tested with fork.

■ Transfer fish to platter; keep warm. Stir cornstarch mixture and bok choy leaves into skillet. Over high heat, cook until mixture boils and thickens, stirring constantly. Spoon over fish.

Makes 4 servings.

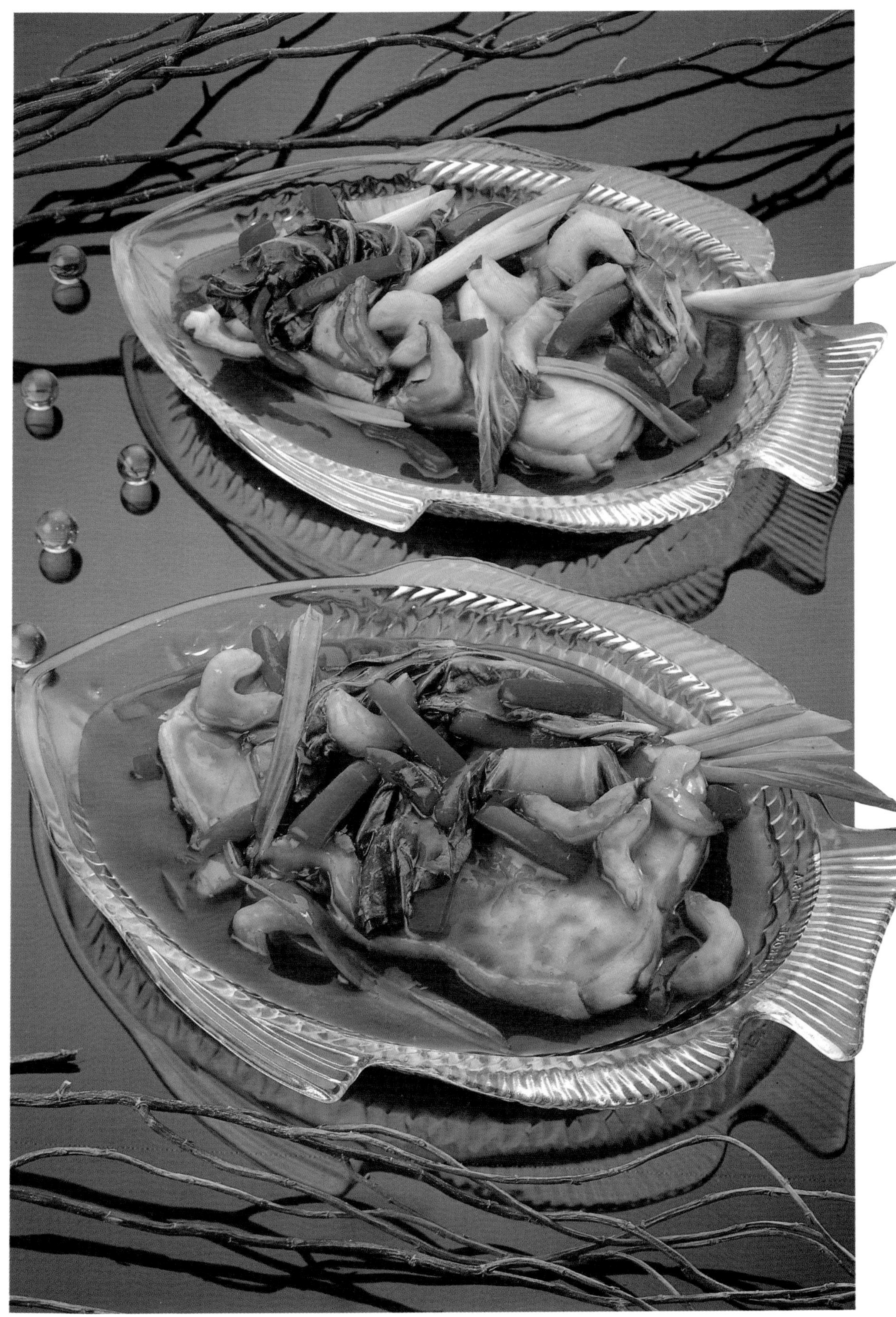

COD STEAKS ORIENTAL

CHEESY TUNA AND TWISTS

8 oz	**(*225 g*) *uncooked* corkscrew macaroni**
2 tbsp	**(*30 mL*) margarine *or* butter**
1 pkg (10 oz)	**(*285 g*) frozen mixed vegetables, thawed**
1	**clove garlic, minced**
1 can	**CAMPBELL'S condensed Cream of Mushroom Soup**
¾ cup	**(*175 mL*) milk**
1½ cups	**(*375 mL*) shredded mozzarella cheese (6 oz / *180 g*)**
⅛ tsp	**(*0,5 mL*) pepper**
	Generous dash ground nutmeg
1 can (6½ oz)	**(*185 g*) tuna, drained**

■ Cook macaroni according to package directions; drain.

■ Meanwhile, in 10-inch (*25 cm*) skillet over medium heat, in hot margarine, cook mixed vegetables and garlic 2 minutes, stirring often.

■ Add soup to skillet; stir until smooth. Gradually stir in milk. Add cheese, pepper and nutmeg; heat until cheese melts, stirring occasionally.

■ Stir in tuna and cooked macaroni. Heat through.

TIP: For a heartier cheese flavor, use sharp Cheddar instead of mozzarella.

Makes about 6 cups (1,5 L) or 4 servings.

1 Cook vegetables and garlic in hot margarine.

2 Add soup to skillet and mix well.

CHEESY TUNA AND TWISTS

3 Gradually stir in milk. Add cheese, pepper and nutmeg.

4 Stir in tuna and cooked macaroni.

FETTUCINI WITH MUSHROOM-CLAM SAUCE

FETTUCINI WITH MUSHROOM-CLAM SAUCE

2 cans (6½ oz *each*)	**(*370 g*) chopped clams**
1 tbsp	**(*15 mL*) margarine *or* butter**
2	**cloves garlic, minced**
¼ cup	**(*50 mL*) Chablis *or* other dry white wine**
1 can	**CAMPBELL'S condensed Cream of Mushroom Soup**
¼ cup	**(*50 mL*) grated Parmesan cheese**
	Hot cooked fettucini
	Chopped fresh parsley for garnish

■ Drain clams, reserving liquid. In 2-quart (*2 L*) saucepan over medium heat, in hot margarine, cook garlic until golden, stirring often.

■ Add clam liquid and wine. Increase heat to high. Boil 6 minutes or until liquid is reduced to *½ cup (125 mL)*.

■ Stir in soup, clams and cheese. Reduce heat to low. Cook 3 minutes or until heated through, stirring occasionally. Serve over fettucini. Garnish with parsley, if desired.

TIP: Look for fresh or refrigerated pasta at your supermarket—most cook in 5 minutes or less. You'll need about 8 ounces (*225 g*) pasta for 4 servings.

Makes 4 servings.

FISH WITH SWISS CHEESE SAUCE

6	**flounder fillets, each cut about ¼ inch (*0,5 cm*) thick (about 1½ lb / *675 g*)**
1 can	**CAMPBELL'S condensed Cream of Mushroom Soup**
2 tbsp	**(*30 mL*) Chablis *or* other white wine**
½ cup	**(*125 mL*) shredded Swiss *or* Emmental cheese (2 oz / *60 g*)**
1 tbsp	**(*15 mL*) chopped fresh parsley**

■ Preheat oven to 400 °F (*200 °C*). In 13- by 9-inch (*33 x 23 cm*) baking dish, arrange fish fillets in a single layer. Bake 10 minutes.

■ Meanwhile, in small bowl, combine soup and wine. Pour soup mixture over fillets, stirring into cooking liquid. Sprinkle with cheese and parsley. Bake 5 minutes more or until fish flakes easily when tested with fork.

Makes 6 servings.

SAUCY CHEESE TORTELLINI

1 lb	**(*450 g*) fresh *or* frozen cheese-filled tortellini***
1 can	**CAMPBELL'S condensed Cream of Mushroom Soup**
1 soup can	**milk**
¾ cup	**(*175 mL*) frozen peas**
½ cup	**(*125 mL*) shredded carrot**
⅛ tsp	**(*0,5 mL*) freshly ground pepper**
3 tbsp	**(*45 mL*) grated Parmesan cheese**
¼ cup	**(*50 mL*) chopped fresh parsley**
	Chopped toasted walnuts for garnish

■ Cook tortellini according to package directions; drain.

■ Meanwhile, in 3-quart (*3 L*) saucepan, combine soup, milk, peas, carrot and pepper. Over medium heat, heat to boiling. Reduce heat to low. Cover; cook 4 minutes or until peas are tender, stirring occasionally.

■ Stir in cheese and parsley. Heat until cheese melts. Stir in cooked tortellini. Garnish with walnuts, if desired.

** If not available at your food market, substitute 3 cups (750 mL) cooked and drained corkscrew macaroni.*

Makes about 5 cups (1,3 L) or 4 main-dish servings.

EGGS DIJON WITH ASPARAGUS

1 pkg (10 oz)	**(*285 g*) frozen asparagus *or* broccoli spears, cut up**
1 can	**CAMPBELL'S condensed Cream of Chicken Soup**
½ cup	**(*125 mL*) milk**
½ tsp	**(*2 mL*) dry mustard**
	Generous dash pepper
4	**hard-cooked eggs, coarsely chopped**
1 cup	**(*250 mL*) shredded Swiss *or* Emmental cheese (4 oz / *120 g*)**
4	**English muffins, split and toasted *or* 8 slices bread, toasted**

■ In covered 2-quart (*2 L*) saucepan over medium heat, in 1 inch (*2,5 cm*) boiling water, cook asparagus 3 minutes. Drain in colander.

■ Meanwhile, in 1½-quart (*1,5 L*) saucepan, combine soup, milk, mustard and pepper. Add eggs and cheese. Over medium heat, heat through, stirring occasionally.

■ On *each* of 4 plates, place 2 muffin halves; top with asparagus and spoon over egg mixture.

Makes 4 servings.

CHEESY MUSHROOM FRITTATA

1 can	**CAMPBELL'S condensed Cream of Mushroom Soup**
6	**eggs, slightly beaten**
1½ cups	**(*375 mL*) shredded mozzarella cheese (6 oz / *180 g*), divided**
¼ tsp	**(*1 mL*) dried basil leaves, crushed**
⅛ tsp	**(*0,5 mL*) pepper**
2 tbsp	**(*30 mL*) margarine *or* butter**
1 cup	**(*250 mL*) sliced fresh mushrooms**
1	**medium onion, chopped**
	Chopped fresh parsley, tomato wedges *and* fresh basil leaves for garnish

■ In medium bowl with wire whisk, beat soup until smooth. Gradually blend in eggs, *1 cup* (*250 mL*) of cheese, basil and pepper.

■ In 10-inch (*25 cm*) *oven-safe* omelet pan or skillet over medium heat, in hot margarine, cook mushrooms and onion until mushrooms are tender and liquid is evaporated, stirring occasionally.

■ Pour mixture into skillet. Reduce heat to low. Cook 6 minutes or until eggs are set 1 inch (*2,5 cm*) from edge. *Do not stir.* Remove from heat.

■ Broil 6 inches (*15 cm*) from heat 5 minutes or until frittata is puffy and lightly browned. Top with remaining cheese. Cover; let stand 2 minutes or until cheese melts. Garnish with parsley, tomato wedges and fresh basil, if desired.

Makes 5 main-dish servings.

CHEESY MUSHROOM FRITTATA

THREE-CHEESE VEGETABLE LASAGNA

2 tbsp	**(*30 mL*) water**
2 pkg (10 oz *each*)	**(*570 g*) frozen chopped broccoli (4 cups / *1 L*)**
1 pkg (10 oz)	**(*285 g*) frozen sliced carrots (2 cups / *500 mL*)**
1 tsp	**(*5 mL*) Italian seasoning, crushed**
¼ tsp	**(*1 mL*) garlic powder**
2 cans	**CAMPBELL'S condensed Cream of Celery *or* Cream of Mushroom Soup**
¾ cup	**(*175 mL*) grated Parmesan cheese, divided**
¾ cup	**(*175 mL*) ricotta cheese**
2 cups	**(*500 mL*) shredded mozzarella cheese (8 oz / *225 g*)**
9	**lasagna noodles, cooked and drained (8 oz / *225 g* uncooked)**
	Paprika

■ In covered 10-inch (*25 cm*) skillet, combine water, broccoli, carrots, Italian seasoning and garlic powder. Heat to boiling. Reduce heat to low. Cover; cook 10 minutes or until vegetables are thawed, stirring occasionally. Drain.

■ Meanwhile, in large bowl, combine soup, *½ cup* (*125 mL*) of Parmesan, ricotta and mozzarella cheese. Reserve *1 cup* (*250 mL*) of cheese mixture. Stir vegetables into remaining cheese mixture.

■ In 12- by 8-inch (*30 x 20 cm*) baking dish, arrange 3 lasagna noodles; spread with ½ of vegetable mixture. Arrange 3 more noodles over filling; spread with remaining vegetable mixture. Top with remaining 3 noodles and reserved cheese mixture. Sprinkle with remaining Parmesan and paprika.

■ Cover with foil. Bake at 375 °F (*190 °C*) for 30 minutes. Uncover; bake 10 minutes more. Let stand 10 minutes before serving.

Makes 8 main-dish servings.

THREE-CHEESE VEGETABLE LASAGNA

GINGERED VEGETABLES

1 tbsp	**(*15 mL*) vegetable oil**
1 cup	**(*250 mL*) diagonally sliced carrots**
1 cup	**(*250 mL*) diagonally sliced celery**
1 cup	**(*250 mL*) sweet red pepper strips**
1 cup	**(*250 mL*) coarsely chopped onion**
1 cup	**(*250 mL*) broccoli flowerets**
1 cup	**(*250 mL*) snow peas**
1	**clove garlic, minced**
½ tsp	**(*2 mL*) ground ginger**
2 tbsp	**(*30 mL*) cornstarch (cornflour)**
1 can	**CAMPBELL'S condensed Chicken Broth**

■ In 10-inch (*25 cm*) skillet or wok over high heat, in hot oil, stir-fry carrots, celery, red pepper and onion 3 minutes.

■ Add broccoli, snow peas, garlic and ginger. Sprinkle cornstarch over vegetables. Stir in broth. Cook until mixture boils and thickens, stirring often. Reduce heat to low. Cover; simmer until vegetables are tender-crisp.

■ Serve with *soy sauce*, if desired.

To microwave: Omit oil. In 3-quart (*3 L*) microwave-safe casserole, combine vegetables and garlic. Cover with lid; microwave on HIGH 7 minutes or until vegetables are tender-crisp, stirring once during cooking. Sprinkle cornstarch over vegetables. Stir in ginger and broth until blended. Cover; microwave on HIGH 4 minutes or until thickened, stirring halfway through cooking. Serve as directed above.

Makes about 4 cups (1 L) or 4 servings.

1 Stir-fry carrots, celery, red pepper and onion.

GINGERED VEGETABLES

2 Add broccoli, snow peas, garlic and ginger.

3 Sprinkle cornstarch over vegetables.

4 Stir in broth and cook until mixture boils.

QUICK RICE AND BEANS

3	**slices bacon, diced**
1	**clove garlic, minced**
¼ tsp	***(1 mL)* ground coriander**
⅛ tsp	***(0,5 mL)* ground cumin**
1 cup	***(250 mL) uncooked* regular rice**
½ cup	***(125 mL)* drained canned chick peas (garbanzo beans), kidney beans *or* pinto beans**
1 can	**CAMPBELL'S condensed Beef Broth** *
½ cup	***(125 mL)* water**
1	**bay leaf**
	Generous dash pepper

** CAMPBELL'S condensed Consommé (Beef) in the U.K.*

■ In 2-quart (*2 L*) saucepan over medium-high heat, cook bacon until crisp. Spoon off fat. Add garlic, coriander and cumin. Cook 1 minute, stirring constantly.

■ Stir in rice, chick peas, broth, water, bay leaf and pepper. Heat to boiling. Reduce heat to low. Cover; simmer 20 minutes or until rice is tender and liquid is absorbed. Remove bay leaf; discard. Garnish with fresh *bay leaves,* if desired.

Makes about 4 cups (1 L) or 8 servings.

TOMATO ZUCCHINI MEDLEY

1 can	**CAMPBELL'S condensed Tomato Soup**
¼ cup	**(*50 mL*) grated Parmesan cheese**
1 tbsp	**(*15 mL*) lemon juice**
½ tsp	**(*2 mL*) garlic powder**
½ tsp	**(*2 mL*) dried basil leaves, crushed**
6 cups	**(*1,5 L*) sliced zucchini (about 1½ lb / *675 g*)**
1	**medium onion, thinly sliced**
1	**green pepper, cut into strips**

■ In large bowl, combine soup, cheese, lemon juice, garlic powder and basil. Add zucchini, onion and green pepper. Toss to coat well.

■ Spoon vegetable mixture into 10-inch (*25 cm*) skillet. Over medium heat, heat to boiling. Reduce heat to low. Cover; cook 10 minutes or until vegetables are tender, stirring occasionally. Top with additional Parmesan cheese, if desired.

To microwave: In 12- by 8-inch (*30 x 20 cm*) microwave-safe baking dish, combine ingredients as directed above. Cover with waxed paper. Microwave on HIGH 15 minutes, stirring halfway through cooking. Continue as directed above.

Makes 8 servings.

CURRY-SAUCED CAULIFLOWER

CURRY-SAUCED CAULIFLOWER

4 cups	**(*1 L*) cauliflowerets**
1 can	**CAMPBELL'S condensed Cream of Celery *or* Cream of Mushroom Soup**
½ cup	**(*125 mL*) milk**
½ cup	**(*125 mL*) shredded Cheddar cheese (2 oz / *60 g*)**
½ tsp	**(*2 mL*) curry powder**
	Generous dash black pepper
1 cup	**(*250 mL*) frozen peas, thawed**
½ cup	**(*125 mL*) diced sweet red pepper**
	Toasted sliced almonds for garnish

■ In covered 10-inch (*25 cm*) skillet over medium heat, in ½ inch (*1 cm*) boiling water, cook cauliflower 5 minutes or until tender-crisp. Drain in colander.

■ In same skillet, combine soup, milk, cheese, curry and black pepper. Add cooked cauliflower, peas and red pepper. Over medium heat, cook 5 minutes or until vegetables are tender, stirring often. Garnish with almonds.

To microwave: In 2-quart (*2 L*) microwave-safe casserole, place cauliflower in ½ inch (*1 cm*) water. Cover with lid; microwave on HIGH 10 minutes or until tender-crisp. Drain in colander. In same casserole, stir soup, milk, cheese, curry and black pepper until smooth. Add cooked cauliflower, peas and red pepper. Cover; microwave on HIGH 3 minutes or until vegetables are tender and cheese melts, stirring once during cooking. Garnish as directed above.

TIP: A great make-ahead recipe—just reheat in your microwave oven.

Makes about 5 cups (1,3 L) or 10 servings.

Creamy Mushroom Pilaf

2 tbsp	**(*30 mL*) margarine *or* butter**
1	**small onion, chopped**
1 cup	**(*250 mL*) sliced fresh mushrooms**
1 cup	**(*250 mL*) *uncooked* regular long-grain rice**
1 can	**CAMPBELL'S condensed Chicken Broth**
¾ cup	**(*175 mL*) water**
¼ cup	**(*50 mL*) Chablis *or* other dry white wine**
¼ tsp	**(*1 mL*) pepper**
¼ cup	**(*50 mL*) sour cream**
½ cup	**(*125 mL*) freshly grated Parmesan cheese (2 oz / *60 g*), divided**
1 tbsp	**(*15 mL*) chopped fresh parsley for garnish**

■ In 2-quart (*2 L*) saucepan over medium heat, in hot margarine, cook onion, mushrooms and rice 5 minutes or until rice is lightly browned, stirring often.

■ Stir in broth, water, wine and pepper. Heat to boiling. Reduce heat to low. Cover; cook 20 minutes. Remove from heat.

■ Stir in sour cream and ¼ cup (*50 mL*) of cheese. Cover; let stand 5 minutes or until all liquid is absorbed. Garnish with remaining ¼ cup (*50 mL*) cheese and parsley.

To microwave: Place margarine in 2-quart (*2 L*) microwave-safe casserole, microwave on HIGH 1 minute until melted. Stir in onion, mushrooms and rice. Microwave on HIGH 5 minutes until rice is lightly browned, stirring once during cooking. Stir in broth, water, wine and pepper; cover with lid. Microwave on HIGH 6 to 8 minutes until mixture is boiling rapidly. Microwave at 50% power 12 minutes until rice is tender but firm. Continue as directed above.

Makes about 4 cups (1 L) or 6 servings.

1 Cook onion, mushrooms and rice for 5 minutes.

2 Rice will become a light brown color.

CREAMY MUSHROOM PILAF

3 Stir in broth, water, wine and pepper.

4 Stir in sour cream and ¼ cup (*50 mL*) of cheese.

Broth-Simmered Rice

1 can	**CAMPBELL'S condensed Chicken *or* Beef Broth***
1 soup can	**water**
1 cup	**(*250 mL*) *uncooked* regular long-grain rice**

** CAMPBELL'S condensed Consommé (Beef) in the U.K.*

In 2-quart (*2 L*) saucepan over medium-high heat, heat chicken broth and water to boiling. Stir in rice. Reduce heat to low. Cover; cook 20 minutes or until rice is tender and liquid is absorbed.

Makes about 3 cups (750 mL) or 6 servings.

Shortcut Chicken Gravy

3 tbsp	**(*45 mL*) margarine *or* butter**
3 tbsp	**(*45 mL*) all-purpose flour**
1 can	**CAMPBELL'S condensed Chicken Broth**
½ cup	**(*125 mL*) milk**

In 2-quart (*2 L*) saucepan over medium heat, melt margarine; add flour. Cook 1 minute, stirring constantly. Gradually stir in broth and milk. Cook until gravy boils and thickens, stirring constantly.

Shortcut Beef Gravy: Prepare Shortcut Chicken Gravy as directed above, *except* substitute 1 can CAMPBELL'S condensed *Beef Broth* * for the chicken broth.

Makes about 2 cups (500 mL) or 16 servings.

** CAMPBELL'S condensed Consommé (Beef) in the U.K.*

VEGETABLE COUSCOUS

1 can	**CAMPBELL'S condensed Chicken Broth**
1½ cups	**(*375 mL*) *uncooked* couscous**
2 tbsp	**(*30 mL*) vegetable oil**
1 cup	**(*250 mL*) sliced fresh mushrooms**
1 cup	**(*250 mL*) chopped onions**
1 cup	**(*250 mL*) shredded carrots**
1 tsp	**(*5 mL*) grated fresh ginger**
2	**cloves garlic, sliced *or* minced**
1 tbsp	**(*15 mL*) soy sauce**
1 tbsp	**(*15 mL*) lemon juice**

■ In 2-quart (*2 L*) saucepan over high heat, heat broth to boiling. Remove from heat. Stir in couscous. Cover; let stand 5 minutes.

■ Meanwhile, in 10-inch (*25 cm*) skillet over medium heat, in hot oil, cook mushrooms, onions, carrots, ginger and garlic until vegetables are tender-crisp, stirring often. Stir in soy sauce and lemon juice.

■ Add couscous. Heat through.

TIP: Reheat leftover vegetable couscous in your microwave oven. Stir in 1 or 2 tablespoons (*15 or 30 mL*) water, if needed.

Makes about 5 cups (1,3 L) or 10 servings.

BULGUR WITH BASIL AND WALNUTS

1 can	**CAMPBELL'S condensed Chicken Broth**
1	**medium onion, chopped**
1 cup	**(*250 mL*) shredded carrots**
2 tbsp	**(*30 mL*) margarine *or* butter**
1	**clove garlic, sliced *or* minced**
1 tsp	**(*5 mL*) dried basil leaves, crushed**
1¼ cups	**(*300 mL*) *uncooked* bulgur wheat**
⅓ cup	**(*75 mL*) chopped walnuts**
1 tbsp	**(*15 mL*) lemon juice**

■ In 2-quart (*2 L*) saucepan over medium heat, combine broth, onion, carrots, margarine, garlic and basil. Heat to boiling.

■ Stir in bulgur, walnuts and lemon juice. Remove from heat. Cover; let stand 15 minutes or until liquid is absorbed.

Makes about 4 cups (1 L) or 8 servings.

MUSHROOM, PEPPER AND ONION SAUCE

1 tbsp	**(*15 mL*) vegetable oil**
1	**medium onion, cut into wedges**
1	**green pepper, cut into thin strips**
¼ tsp	**(*1 mL*) dried thyme leaves, crushed**
1 can	**CAMPBELL'S condensed Cream of Mushroom Soup**
½ cup	**(*125 mL*) water**

■ In 1½-quart (*1,5 L*) saucepan over medium heat, in hot oil, cook onion, pepper and thyme until vegetables are tender.

■ Stir in soup and water. Cook 5 minutes. Serve over grilled or broiled steak.

Makes about 2½ cups (625 mL).

BULGUR WITH BASIL AND WALNUTS

Curried Peanut Rice

2 tbsp	**(*30 mL*) vegetable oil**
¼ cup	**(*50 mL*) sliced green onions (spring onions)**
2 tsp	**(*10 mL*) curry powder**
1 can	**CAMPBELL'S condensed Chicken Broth**
½ cup	**(*125 mL*) frozen peas**
1¼ cups	**(*300 mL*) *uncooked* quick-cooking rice**
½ cup	**(*125 mL*) coarsely chopped unsalted roasted peanuts**

■ In 2-quart (*2 L*) saucepan over medium heat, in hot oil, cook green onions and curry powder until onions are tender, stirring occasionally.

■ Add broth and peas. Heat to boiling. Add rice. Remove from heat. Cover; let stand 5 minutes or until most of the liquid is absorbed. Stir in peanuts. Fluff with fork before serving.

Makes about 2½ cups (625 mL) or 5 servings.

MUSHROOMS IN GARLIC SAUCE

2 tbsp	**(*30 mL*) olive oil**
1	**medium onion, sliced**
4	**cloves garlic, minced**
½ tsp	**(*2 mL*) chopped fresh rosemary *or* ¼ tsp (*1 mL*) dried rosemary leaves, crushed**
¼ tsp	**(*1 mL*) dried thyme leaves, crushed**
1½ lb	**(*675 g*) fresh mushrooms, thinly sliced**
1 can	**CAMPBELL'S condensed French Onion Soup ***
1 tsp	**(*5 mL*) lime juice**
¼ cup	**(*50 mL*) dry white wine *or* dry sherry**
	Chopped fresh parsley

* *Not available in the U.K.*

■ In 6-quart (*6 L*) Dutch oven over medium heat, in hot oil, cook onion, garlic, rosemary and thyme until onion is tender.

■ Increase heat to medium-high. Add mushrooms. Cook until mushrooms begin to brown. Add soup and lime juice. Heat to boiling. Reduce heat to low. Cook until mushrooms are tender, stirring occasionally.

■ Add wine. Cook 3 minutes. Sprinkle with parsley. Garnish with fresh *rosemary* and *lime slice*, if desired. Serve with meat, rice or noodles.

Makes about 2¾ cups (675 mL) or 6 servings.

MUSHROOM MORNAY SAUCE

1 can	**CAMPBELL'S condensed Cream of Mushroom Soup**
¾ cup	**(*175 mL*) milk**
¼ tsp	**(*1 mL*) dry mustard**
1	**egg**
½ cup	**(*125 mL*) shredded Swiss *or* Emmental cheese**
1 tbsp	**(*15 mL*) grated Parmesan cheese**
	Desired hot cooked vegetables

■ In 1½-quart (*1,5 L*) saucepan, stir soup; stir in milk and mustard until smooth. Over medium heat, heat through, stirring occasionally.

■ In small cup, lightly beat egg. Stir some hot soup mixture into beaten egg. Stir egg mixture back into soup in saucepan.

■ Over low heat, cook until mixture thickens, stirring constantly. *Do not boil.* Remove from heat. Stir in Swiss and Parmesan. Cook until cheese melts. Serve over vegetables.

Makes about 2 cups (500 mL).

1 Pour soup into saucepan and stir. Stir in milk and mustard until smooth.

2 Cook, uncovered, over medium heat, stirring occasionally.

3 Beat egg in small cup and add some of hot soup mixture.

4 Stir egg mixture into soup in saucepan.

BROCCOLI BAKE

1 can	**CAMPBELL'S condensed Cream of Broccoli *or* Cream of Mushroom Soup**
½ cup	**(*125 mL*) milk**
1 tsp	**(*5 mL*) soy sauce**
	Dash pepper
5 cups	**(*1,3 L*) fresh broccoli flowerets (about 1½ lb / *675 g*), cooked and drained**
1 can (2.8 oz)	**(*79 g*) French fried onions, divided***

■ In 10- by 6-inch (*25 x 15 cm*) baking dish, combine soup, milk, soy sauce and pepper. Stir in broccoli and *½ can* of onions.

■ Bake, uncovered, at 350 °F (*180 °C*) for 25 minutes. Top with remaining onions. Bake 5 minutes more.

TIP: If you like, substitute one package (20 ounces / *570 g*) frozen *broccoli cuts,* cooked and drained, for the fresh broccoli.

** If not available at your food market, stir ½ cup (125 mL) chopped green onions (spring onions) into soup mixture along with broccoli. Continue as directed. Sprinkle with 2 tablespoons (30 mL) toasted sliced almonds before serving.*

Makes about 4½ cups (1,1 L) or 6 servings.

BROCCOLI-RICE CASSEROLE

BROCCOLI-RICE CASSEROLE

1 tbsp	**(*15 mL*) vegetable oil**
½ cup	**(*125 mL*) chopped celery**
¼ cup	**(*50 mL*) chopped onion**
1 can	**CAMPBELL'S condensed Cream of Broccoli *or* Cream of Mushroom Soup**
¼ cup	**(*50 mL*) milk**
1 cup	**(*250 mL*) pasteurized process cheese spread* cut in ¼-inch (*0,5 cm*) cubes (6 oz / *180 g*)**
1 pkg (10 oz)	**(*285 g*) frozen chopped broccoli, thawed and drained**
1 can (8 oz)	**(*225 g*) sliced water chestnuts, drained**
2 cups	**(*500 mL*) cooked regular rice**
	Paprika

■ Preheat oven to 350 °F (*180 °C*). In 1½-quart (*1,5 L*) saucepan over medium heat, in hot oil, cook celery and onion until tender-crisp, stirring occasionally. Stir in soup and milk.

■ In 10- by 6-inch (*25 x 15 cm*) baking dish, place cheese, broccoli, water chestnuts and rice. Stir in soup mixture. Sprinkle with paprika. Bake 30 minutes or until hot and bubbling.

To microwave: Omit oil. In 10- by 6-inch (*25 x 15 cm*) microwave-safe baking dish, combine celery and onion. Cover with vented plastic wrap; microwave on HIGH 3 minutes. Stir in soup and milk. Add cheese, broccoli, water chestnuts and rice, stirring to mix. Sprinkle with paprika. Microwave, uncovered, on HIGH 10 minutes, rotating dish halfway through cooking.

** If not available at your food market, omit process cheese spread and substitute 1½ cups (375 mL) shredded Cheddar cheese (6 oz / 180 g).*

Makes about 5 cups (1,3 L) or 8 servings.

VEGETABLES WITH BROCCOLI LEMON SAUCE

3 lb	**(*1,4 kg*) small red potatoes, quartered**
2 cups	**(*500 mL*) broccoli flowerets**
1	**large sweet red pepper, cut into ½-inch (*1 cm*) slices**
1 can	**CAMPBELL's condensed Cream of Broccoli, Cream of Celery *or* Cream of Mushroom Soup**
½ cup	**(*125 mL*) mayonnaise**
¼ cup	**(*50 mL*) finely chopped green onions (spring onions)**
1 tbsp	**(*15 mL*) lemon juice**
¼ tsp	**(*1 mL*) dried thyme leaves, crushed**

■ In 6-quart (*6 L*) Dutch oven fitted with steamer basket, over high heat, heat 1 inch (*2,5 cm*) water to boiling. Arrange potatoes in even layer in basket. Cover and steam potatoes 10 minutes. Add broccoli and red pepper; steam vegetables 5 minutes more or until tender.

■ Meanwhile, in 2-quart (*2 L*) saucepan over medium heat, combine soup, mayonnaise, onions, lemon juice and thyme. Heat through, stirring occasionally. Pour over vegetables.

Makes 8 servings.

1 Arrange potatoes in even layer in basket. Steam 10 minutes.

2 Add broccoli and red pepper.

3 Heat soup mixture and pour over vegetables.

VEGETABLES WITH BROCCOLI LEMON SAUCE

SOUPER CHICKEN TETRAZZINI

8 oz	**(*225 g*) *uncooked* spaghetti**
2 tbsp	**(*30 mL*) margarine *or* butter**
2 cups	**(*500 mL*) sliced fresh mushrooms**
1	**small onion, chopped**
2 cans	**CAMPBELL'S condensed Cream of Chicken Soup**
1 soup can	**milk**
2 tbsp	**(*30 mL*) dry sherry**
2 cups	**(*500 mL*) cubed cooked chicken**
⅓ cup	**(*75 mL*) grated Parmesan cheese**
¼ cup	**(*50 mL*) chopped fresh parsley**

■ In 6-quart (*6 L*) Dutch oven, cook spaghetti according to package directions; drain.

■ Meanwhile, in 2-quart (*2 L*) saucepan over medium heat, in hot margarine, cook mushrooms and onion until tender, stirring occasionally. Stir in soup, milk and sherry; heat through.

■ Return cooked spaghetti to Dutch oven. Add soup mixture, chicken, Parmesan and parsley. Toss lightly until spaghetti is coated. Over medium heat, heat through. Serve with additional *Parmesan*, if desired.

Makes about 6 cups (1,5 L) or 4 main-dish servings.

EASY BARBECUE SAUCE

1 can	**CAMPBELL'S condensed Tomato Soup**
⅓ cup	**(*75 mL*) Worcestershire sauce**
3 tbsp	**(*45 mL*) vinegar**
2 tbsp	**(*30 mL*) packed brown sugar**
1	**small onion, chopped**

In 1-quart (*1 L*) saucepan, combine soup, Worcestershire, vinegar, sugar and onion. Over medium heat, heat to boiling. Reduce heat to low. Cook 10 minutes. Use to baste beef or chicken during broiling or grilling.

Makes about 1¾ cups (425 mL) sauce.

SOUPER CHICKEN TETRAZZINI

SIMPLE SALISBURY STEAK

SIMPLE SALISBURY STEAK

1 can	**CAMPBELL'S condensed Cream of Mushroom Soup, divided**
1 lb	**(*450 g*) ground beef**
⅓ cup	**(*75 mL*) dry bread crumbs**
¼ cup	**(*50 mL*) finely chopped onion**
1	**egg, beaten**
	Vegetable cooking spray
1½ cups	**(*375 mL*) sliced fresh mushrooms**
	Fresh parsley and cherry tomatoes for garnish

■ In large bowl, mix thoroughly *¼ cup (50 mL)* of soup, the beef, bread crumbs, onion and egg. Shape firmly into 6 oval patties of even thickness.

■ Spray 10-inch (*25 cm*) skillet with cooking spray. Over medium-high heat, cook *half* of patties, until browned on both sides. Remove; set aside. Repeat with remaining patties. Spoon off fat.

■ In same skillet, stir in remaining soup and mushrooms; return patties to skillet. Reduce heat to low. Cover; cook 20 minutes or until patties are thoroughly cooked and no longer pink, turning patties occasionally. Serve with mushroom sauce. Garnish with parsley and cherry tomatoes, if desired.

Turkey Salisbury Steak: Prepare Simple Salisbury Steak as directed above, *except* substitute 1 pound (*450 g*) ground *raw turkey* for the beef, and increase *dry bread crumbs* to ½ cup (*125 mL*).

TIP: You can substitute 1 can (about 6 ounces / *180 mL*) sliced mushrooms and ¼ cup (*50 mL*) of mushroom liquid or water for the fresh mushrooms in this recipe.

Makes 6 main-dish servings.

GLORIFIED PORK CHOPS

1 tbsp	**(*15 mL*) vegetable oil**
6	**pork chops, each cut ¾ inch (*2 cm*) thick (about 2 lb / *900 g*)**
1 can	**CAMPBELL'S condensed Cream of Celery *or* Cream of Mushroom Soup**
¼ cup	**(*50 mL*) water**
	Sliced tomato and fresh parsley sprigs for garnish

■ In 10-inch (*25 cm*) skillet over medium-high heat, in hot oil, cook chops, *half* at a time, 10 minutes or until browned on both sides. Remove; set aside. Repeat with remaining chops. Spoon off fat.

■ Add soup and water to skillet; stir until smooth. Heat to boiling. Return chops to skillet. Reduce heat to low. Cover; cook 10 minutes or until chops are fork-tender, stirring occasionally. Garnish with tomato and parsley, if desired.

Onion Glorified Pork Chops: Prepare Glorified Pork Chops as directed above, *except* cook 1 medium *onion*, sliced, along with chops.

Savory Glorified Pork Chops: Prepare Glorified Pork Chops as directed above, *except* add 1 teaspoon (*5 mL*) *Worcestershire sauce* along with soup.

Mushroom Glorified Pork Chops: Prepare Glorified Pork Chops as directed above, using the *Cream of Mushroom Soup*. Add 1 can (about 6 ounces / *180 mL*) *sliced mushrooms*, drained, along with soup.

Makes 6 main-dish servings.

1 Cook pork chops in hot oil.

2 Turn chops over to brown both sides.

GLORIFIED PORK CHOPS

3 Spoon off fat from skillet.

4 Add soup mixture and return chops to skillet.

LEMON-BROCCOLI CHICKEN

1	**lemon**
1 tbsp	**(*15 mL*) vegetable oil**
4	**skinless, boneless chicken breast halves (about 1 lb / *450 g*)**
1 can	**CAMPBELL'S condensed Cream of Broccoli *or* Cream of Mushroom Soup**
1/4 cup	**(*50 mL*) milk**
1/8 tsp	**(*0,5 mL*) pepper**
	Fresh marjoram sprigs and carrot curls for garnish

■ Cut 4 thin slices from lemon; set slices aside. Squeeze *2 teaspoons* (*10 mL*) juice from remaining lemon; set aside.

■ In 10-inch (*25 cm*) skillet over medium-high heat, in hot oil, cook chicken 10 minutes or until browned on both sides. Spoon off fat.

■ Meanwhile, in small bowl, combine soup and milk. Stir in reserved lemon juice and pepper; pour over chicken. Top each chicken piece with lemon slice.

■ Reduce heat to low. Cover; cook 5 minutes or until chicken is no longer pink, stirring occasionally. Garnish with marjoram and carrot curls, if desired.

Lemon-Broccoli Turkey: Prepare Lemon Broccoli Chicken as directed above, *except* substitute 4 *raw turkey cutlets* (about 1 pound / *450 g*) for the chicken. Cook turkey about 8 minutes until turkey is browned and no longer pink. Continue as directed above.

Makes 4 main-dish servings.

LEMON-BROCCOLI CHICKEN

CREAMY MUSHROOM SAUCE

1 can	**CAMPBELL'S condensed Cream of Mushroom Soup**
⅓ cup	**(*75 mL*) milk *or* water**

In 1-quart (*1 L*) saucepan, combine soup and milk. Over medium heat, heat until hot and bubbling, stirring often.

To microwave: In 1-quart (*1 L*) microwave-safe casserole, combine soup and milk. Microwave, uncovered, on HIGH 2½ minutes or until hot and bubbling, stirring halfway through heating.

Makes about 1½ cups (375 mL) sauce or 12 side-dish servings.

SOUPER GRAVY FOR ROAST MEAT OR POULTRY

2 to 4 tbsp	**(*30 to 60 mL*) roasted meat *or* poultry drippings in pan**
1 can	**CAMPBELL'S condensed Cream of Chicken, Cream of Mushroom *or* Cream of Broccoli Soup**
¼ to ⅓ cup	**(*50 to 75 mL*) water**

After roasting meat or poultry, remove roast from pan. Spoon off excess fat, reserving 2 to 4 tablespoons (*30 to 60 mL*) drippings. Stir in soup and water. Over medium heat, heat through, stirring to loosen browned bits. Serve with roast.

Makes about 1½ cups (375 mL).

EASY TURKEY SALAD

1 can — **CAMPBELL'S condensed Cream of Celery Soup**

½ cup — **(*125 mL*) mayonnaise**

4 cups — **(*1 L*) chopped cooked turkey *or* chicken**

1 cup — **(*250 mL*) finely chopped celery**

½ cup — **(*125 mL*) chopped sweet red pepper**

½ cup — **(*125 mL*) sliced green onions (spring onions)**

2 tbsp — **(*30 mL*) chopped fresh parsley**

⅛ tsp — **(*0,5 mL*) pepper**

Leaf lettuce

■ In large bowl, stir together soup and mayonnaise until smooth. Fold in turkey, celery, red pepper, onions, parsley and pepper.

■ Serve mixture on leaf lettuce. Cover and refrigerate any remaining salad mixture.

Makes about 5 cups (1,3 L) or 5 main-dish servings.

SENSATIONAL BEEF STROGANOFF

1 lb	**(*450 g*) boneless beef top round steak, (about ¾ inch / *2 cm* thick)**
2 tbsp	**(*30 mL*) margarine *or* butter, divided**
½ cup	**(*125 mL*) chopped onion**
1 can	**CAMPBELL'S condensed Cream of Mushroom Soup**
½ tsp	**(*2 mL*) paprika**
½ cup	**(*125 mL*) sour cream *or* yogurt**
	Hot cooked noodles
	Chopped fresh parsley, paprika, tomato wedges and fresh savory sprigs for garnish

■ Slice beef across the grain into thin strips.

■ In 10-inch (*25 cm*) skillet over medium-high heat, in *1 tablespoon* (*15 mL*) of hot margarine, cook *half* of beef and *half* of onion until meat is no longer pink and onion is tender; set aside. Repeat with remaining margarine, beef and onion. Spoon off fat.

■ Return meat mixture to skillet. Stir in soup and ½ teaspoon (*2 mL*) paprika. Heat through, stirring occasionally. Remove from heat. Stir in sour cream. Serve over noodles. Sprinkle with parsley and additional paprika. Garnish with tomatoes and savory, if desired.

Turkey Stroganoff: Prepare Sensational Beef Stroganoff as directed above, *except* substitute 1 pound (*450 g*) *raw turkey cutlets* for the beef.

Pork Stroganoff: Prepare Sensational Beef Stroganoff as directed above, *except* substitute 1 pound (*450 g*) boneless *pork loin* for the beef.

TIP: To make slicing the meat easier, freeze beef, turkey or pork about 1 hour before cutting into thin strips.

Makes about 3½ cups (875 mL) or 6 main-dish servings.

1 Slice the beef across the grain into thin strips.

2 Heat margarine in frying pan. When hot, add half of beef and half of onion.

SENSATIONAL BEEF STROGANOFF

3 Remove beef and onion from pan; spoon off fat.

4 Stir in soup and paprika.

CLASSIC POTATO SALAD

9	**medium potatoes (3 lb / *1,4 kg*)**
1 can	**CAMPBELL'S condensed Cream of Celery Soup**
¾ cup	**(*175 mL*) mayonnaise**
2 tbsp	**(*30 mL*) red wine vinegar**
½ tsp	**(*2 mL*) celery seed**
1 cup	**(*250 mL*) chopped celery**
¼ cup	**(*50 mL*) chopped green onions (spring onions)**
½ cup	**(*125 mL*) chopped green pepper**
2	**hard-cooked eggs, chopped**

■ In 4-quart (*4 L*) saucepan, place potatoes; add water to cover. Over high heat, heat to boiling. Reduce heat to low. Cover; cook 20 minutes or until fork-tender; drain. Cool slightly. Peel potatoes; cut into ½-inch (*1 cm*) cubes.

■ In large bowl, combine soup, mayonnaise, vinegar and celery seed.

■ Add potatoes, celery, green onions, green pepper and eggs; toss gently to coat. Cover; refrigerate at least 4 hours before serving.

Makes about 7 cups (1,8 L) or 8 side-dish servings.

CREAMY BAKED MACARONI

1 can	**CAMPBELL'S condensed Cream of Chicken Soup**
1 cup	**(*250 mL*) milk**
1 tbsp	**(*15 mL*) chopped chives**
½ tsp	**(*2 mL*) dry mustard**
¼ tsp	**(*1 mL*) hot pepper sauce**
4 cups	**(*1 L*) cooked elbow macaroni (2 cups / *500 mL* uncooked)**
1½ cups	**(*375 mL*) Gouda cheese cut in ½-inch (*1 cm*) cubes (8 ounces / *225 g*)**
2 tbsp	**(*30 mL*) buttered bread crumbs**

■ Preheat oven to 400 °F (*200 °C*). In 2-quart (*2 L*) casserole, combine soup, milk, chives, mustard and hot pepper sauce.

■ Stir in macaroni and cheese. Sprinkle with bread crumbs. Bake 25 minutes or until hot and bubbly.

Makes about 6 cups (1,5 L) or 6 side-dish servings.

CLASSIC POTATO SALAD

GLORIFIED CHICKEN BAKE

2½- to 3-lb	**(*1,1- to 1,4- kg*) broiler-fryer chicken, cut up**
1 tbsp	**(*15 mL*) margarine *or* butter, melted**
1 can	**CAMPBELL'S condensed Cream of Chicken, Cream of Broccoli, Cream of Celery *or* Cream of Mushroom Soup**
	Fresh rosemary sprigs *and* green and sweet red pepper strips for garnish

■ In 12- by 8-inch (*30 x 20 cm*) baking dish, arrange chicken skin side up. Drizzle with margarine. Bake at 375 °F (*190 °C*) for 40 minutes.

■ Spoon soup over chicken. Bake 20 minutes more or until chicken is no longer pink and juices run clear.

■ To serve, arrange chicken on serving platter. Stir sauce and spoon over chicken. Garnish with rosemary and pepper strips, if desired.

Glorified Chicken Skillet: Use same ingredients as above in Glorified Chicken Bake, *except* omit the margarine. In 10-inch (*25 cm*) skillet over medium-high heat, heat 2 tablespoons (*30 mL*) *vegetable oil* until hot. Cook chicken 10 minutes or until browned on all sides. Spoon off fat. Stir in soup. Reduce heat to low. Cover; cook 35 minutes or until chicken is no longer pink and juices run clear, stirring occasionally.

TIP: Substitute 4 chicken legs (about 2 pounds / *900 g*) for the broiler-fryer chicken.

NOTE: A popular Campbell recipe since 1957, this three-ingredient main dish can be cooked in the oven or on top of the range.

Makes 4 main-dish servings.

1 Arrange chicken pieces, skin-side up, in dish.

2 Drizzle with melted margarine.

GLORIFIED CHICKEN BAKE

3 Bake at 375 °F (*190 °C*) for 40 minutes.

4 Mix soup and pour over chicken.

CLASSIC GREEN BEAN BAKE

1 can	**CAMPBELL'S condensed Cream of Mushroom Soup**
½ cup	**(*125 mL*) milk**
1 tsp	**(*5 mL*) soy sauce**
	Dash pepper
4 cups	**(*1 L*) cooked green beans**
1 can (2.8 oz)	**(*79 g*) French fried onions, divided***

■ In 1½-quart (*1,5 L*) casserole, combine soup, milk, soy sauce and pepper. Stir in green beans and *½ can* onions.

■ Bake at 350 °F (*180 °C*) for 25 minutes or until hot; stir. Top with remaining onions. Bake 5 minutes more.

TIP: Buy 2 packages (about 9 ounces / *250 g each*) frozen cut green beans, 2 cans (about 16 ounces / *450 mL each*) cut green beans or about 1½ pounds (*675 g*) fresh green beans for this recipe.

** If not available at your food market, stir ½ cup (125 mL) chopped green onions (spring onions) into soup mixture along with green beans. Continue as directed. Sprinkle with 2 tablespoons (30 mL) toasted sliced almonds before serving.*

Makes about 4½ cups (1,1 L) or 6 side-dish servings.

CLASSIC SOUPERBURGER

1 lb	**(*450 g*) ground beef**
½ cup	**(*125 mL*) chopped onion**
1 can	**CAMPBELL'S condensed Tomato *or* Cream of Mushroom Soup**
1 tbsp	**(*15 mL*) prepared mustard *or* mild English mustard**
	Dash pepper
6	**hamburger buns, split and toasted**

■ In 10-inch (*25 cm*) skillet over medium heat, cook beef and onion until tender and beef is thoroughly cooked and no longer pink, stirring to separate meat. Spoon off fat.

■ Stir in soup, mustard and pepper. Heat through, stirring occasionally. Serve on buns.

Makes about 2¾ cups (675 mL) or 6 main-dish servings.

CLASSIC GREEN BEAN BAKE (top)
CLASSIC SOUPERBURGER (bottom)

Broiled Shrimp Dijon

1 can	**CAMPBELL'S condensed Tomato Soup**
1	**clove garlic, minced**
2 tbsp	**(*30 mL*) vegetable oil**
1 tbsp	**(*15 mL*) brown sugar**
1 tbsp	**(*15 mL*) Dijon-style mustard**
1 tsp	**(*5 mL*) lemon juice**
½ tsp	**(*2 mL*) hot pepper sauce**
1 lb	**(*450 g*) extra-large shrimp in shells (about 24)**
	Shredded lettuce for garnish

■ *To make marinade:* In 2-quart (*2 L*) saucepan, stir together soup, garlic, oil, sugar, mustard, lemon juice and hot pepper sauce. Over medium heat, cook until mixture boils and sugar is dissolved, stirring occasionally. Remove from heat.

■ Shell and devein shrimp, leaving tails intact. Place in large bowl; add marinade. Cover; refrigerate 2 hours.

■ Remove shrimp from bowl, reserving marinade. Arrange shrimp on rack in broiler pan. Broil 4 inches (*10 cm*) from heat 8 minutes or until shrimp are pink and opaque, turning once and brushing often with marinade.

■ Meanwhile, in 1-quart (*1 L*) saucepan over medium heat, heat remaining marinade to boiling, stirring often.

■ To serve, place shrimp on bed of lettuce, if desired. Serve sauce with shrimp.

Makes about 24 appetizers.

1 Stir together soup, garlic, oil, sugar, mustard, lemon juice and hot pepper sauce.

2 Cook until sugar is dissolved. Remove from heat.

BROILED SHRIMP DIJON

3 Devein shrimp.

4 Baste shrimp with marinade during cooking.

VEGETABLE BEEF SOUP

2 cans	**CAMPBELL'S condensed Beef Broth** *
1 soup can	**water**
2	**medium potatoes, cubed**
1 pkg (16 oz)	**(*450 g*) frozen mixed vegetables**
1 can (about 8 oz)	**(*225 mL*) tomatoes, undrained and cut up**
1 cup	**(*250 mL*) cubed cooked beef**
¼ tsp	**(*1 mL*) dried thyme leaves, crushed**
⅛ tsp	**(*0,5 mL*) pepper**

** CAMPBELL'S condensed Consommé (Beef) in the U.K.*

■ In 3-quart (*3 L*) saucepan, combine broth, water and potatoes. Over high heat, heat to boiling. Reduce heat to low. Cover; cook 5 minutes or until potatoes are tender.

■ Add vegetables, tomatoes, beef, thyme and pepper. Cover; heat to simmering. Cook until vegetables are tender.

TIP: Create your own combination of vegetables to make this savory soup. You'll need a total of 4 cups (*1 L*) of frozen mixed vegetables.

Makes about 7½ cups (1,9 L) or 6 side-dish servings.

CHICKEN NOODLE SOUP

2 cans	**CAMPBELL'S condensed Chicken Broth**
2 soup cans	**water**
¼ cup	**(*50 mL*) chopped celery**
¼ cup	**(*50 mL*) chopped carrot**
1 tbsp	**(*15 mL*) finely chopped onion**
1 tbsp	**(*15 mL*) chopped fresh parsley**
⅛ tsp	**(*0,5 mL*) poultry seasoning**
⅛ tsp	**(*0,5 mL*) dried thyme leaves, crushed**
2 cups	**(*500 mL*) diced cooked chicken *or* turkey**
1 cup	**(*250 mL*) cooked medium egg noodles (1 cup / *250 mL* uncooked)**

■ In 3-quart (*3 L*) saucepan, combine broth, water, celery, carrot, onion, parsley, poultry seasoning and thyme. Over medium heat, heat to boiling, stirring occasionally.

■ Reduce heat to low. Cover; cook 20 minutes or until vegetables are tender, stirring occasionally. Add chicken and noodles; heat through, stirring occasionally.

Makes about 7 cups (1,8 L) or 4 main-dish servings.

CLASSIC TUNA NOODLE CASSEROLE

CLASSIC TUNA NOODLE CASSEROLE

2 tbsp	**(*30 mL*) margarine *or* butter**
½ cup	**(*125 mL*) chopped onion**
1 can	**CAMPBELL'S condensed Cream of Mushroom Soup**
½ cup	**(*125 mL*) milk**
2 cups	**(*500 mL*) cooked medium egg noodles (2 cups / *500 mL* uncooked)**
1 cup	**(*250 mL*) cooked peas**
2 cans (about 7 oz *each*)	**(*400 g*) tuna, drained and flaked**
½ cup	**(*125 mL*) shredded Cheddar cheese**

■ In 2-quart (*2 L*) saucepan over medium heat, in hot margarine, cook onion until tender. Stir in soup, milk, noodles, peas and tuna. Pour into 1½-quart (*1,5 L*) casserole.

■ Bake at 400 °F (*200 °C*) for 25 minutes or until hot; stir. Top with cheese. Bake 5 minutes more or until cheese melts.

Tuna-Tomato Noodle Casserole: Prepare as directed above, *except* add ½ cup (*125 mL*) drained chopped canned *tomatoes* to noodle mixture. Substitute 2 slices (about 2 ounces / *60 g*) process cheese, cut in half diagonally for shredded cheese.

TIP: Substitute a 10- by 6-inch (*25 x 15 cm*) shallow oblong baking dish for 1½-quart (*1,5 L*) casserole. Reduce baking time to 20 minutes before stirring.

Makes about 5½ cups (1,4 L) or 4 main-dish servings.

CREAMY VEGETABLE MEDLEY

1 can	**CAMPBELL'S condensed Cream of Celery *or* Cream of Mushroom Soup**
1 pkg (16 oz)	**(*450 g*) frozen vegetable combination (about 4 cups (*1 L*) vegetables such as: broccoli, carrots and cauliflower)**

■ In 2-quart (*2 L*) saucepan over medium heat, heat soup to boiling. Stir in vegetables.

■ Return to boiling. Reduce heat to low. Cover; cook 10 minutes or until vegetables are tender, stirring occasionally.

To microwave: In 2-quart (*2 L*) microwave-safe casserole, combine soup and vegetables. Cover with lid; microwave on HIGH 10 minutes or until vegetables are tender, stirring halfway through cooking. Let stand covered, 5 minutes.

Makes about 3 cups (750 mL) or 6 side-dish servings.

CLASSIC FAMILY MEAT LOAF

- **1 can** — **CAMPBELL'S condensed Cream of Mushroom *or* Tomato Soup**
- **1½ lb** — **(*675 g*) ground beef**
- **½ cup** — **(*125 mL*) dry bread crumbs**
- **¼ cup** — **(*50 mL*) finely chopped onion**
- **1 tbsp** — **(*15 mL*) Worcestershire sauce**
- **1** — **egg, beaten**
- **⅛ tsp** — **(*0,5 mL*) pepper**
- **¼ cup** — **(*50 mL*) water**

■ In large bowl, mix thoroughly ½ cup (*125 mL*) of soup, beef, bread crumbs, onion, Worcestershire, egg and pepper. In 12- by 8-inch (*30 x 20 cm*) baking pan, *firmly* shape meat into 8- by 4-inch (*20 x 10 cm*) loaf.

■ Bake at 350 °F (*180 °C*) for 1¼ hours or until meat loaf is thoroughly cooked and no pink remains. Spoon off fat, reserving 1 to 2 tablespoons (*15 to 30 mL*) drippings.

■ In 1-quart (*1 L*) saucepan over medium heat, heat remaining soup, water and reserved drippings to boiling, stirring occasionally. Serve sauce with meat loaf.

Makes 6 main-dish servings.

SAVORY CHICKEN-STUFFING BAKE

1 pkg (6 oz)	**(*180 g*) instant chicken-flavored stuffing mix***
6	**skinless, boneless chicken breast halves (about 1½ lb / *675 g*)**
1 can	**CAMPBELL'S condensed Cream of Chicken Soup**
⅓ cup	**(*75 mL*) milk**
1 tbsp	**(*15 mL*) chopped fresh *or* 1 tsp (*5 mL*) dried parsley**
	Paprika *and* watercress sprigs for garnish

■ Preheat oven to 400 °F (*200 °C*). Prepare stuffing mix according to package directions, but *do not let stand* as directed on package.

■ In 12- by 8-inch (*30 x 20 cm*) baking dish, spoon stuffing down center of dish, leaving space on both sides of stuffing to arrange chicken. (Stuffing should run crosswise, not lengthwise, in dish.) Arrange 3 chicken pieces on each side of stuffing, overlapping, if necessary.

■ In bowl, combine soup, milk and parsley. Pour over chicken. Cover with foil; bake 15 minutes. Uncover; bake 10 minutes more or until chicken is no longer pink.

■ To serve, sprinkle with paprika. Stir sauce at edges and spoon over chicken. Garnish with watercress, if desired.

TIP: When you buy chicken, look for a "sell by" label on the package. Most chicken processors specify the last day poultry should be sold. Avoid packages with expired dates.

**If not available at your food market, substitute 4 cups (1 L) herb seasoned croutons (8ounces / 225 g), ½ cup (125 mL) boiling water and 1 tablespoon (15 mL) melted margarine or butter. Toss together in a medium mixing bowl; continue as directed.*

Makes 6 main-dish servings.

1 Spoon stuffing down center of dish.

SAVORY CHICKEN-STUFFING BAKE

2 Arrange 3 chicken pieces on each side of stuffing.

3 In small bowl, combine soup, milk and parsley.

4 Pour soup mixture over chicken.

SWEDISH MEATBALLS

SWEDISH MEATBALLS

1 can	**CAMPBELL'S condensed Cream of Mushroom Soup**
½ cup	**(*125 mL*) water**
¼ cup	**(*50 mL*) sour cream**
1 lb	**(*450 g*) lean ground beef**
½ cup	**(*125 mL*) soft bread crumbs**
¼ cup	**(*50 mL*) finely chopped onion**
1	**egg, beaten**
¼ tsp	**(*1 mL*) ground nutmeg**
2 tbsp	**(*30 mL*) vegetable oil**
	Hot cooked noodles
	Cherry tomatoes *and* fresh parsley for garnish

■ In small bowl, combine soup, water and sour cream; set aside.

■ In medium bowl, mix thoroughly beef, bread crumbs, onion, egg and nutmeg. Shape mixture into 16 meatballs.

■ In 10-inch (*25 cm*) skillet over medium heat, in hot oil, brown meatballs a few at a time until thoroughly cooked and no longer pink. Spoon off fat.

■ Stir in soup mixture. Reduce heat to low. Heat through; *do not boil.* Serve over noodles. Garnish with tomatoes and parsley, if desired.

Makes 4 main-dish servings.

STROGANOFF SAUCE

1 tbsp	**(*15 mL*) margarine *or* butter**
¼ cup	**(*50 mL*) chopped onion**
1 can	**CAMPBELL'S condensed Cream of Mushroom Soup**
⅓ cup	**(*75 mL*) sour cream**
¼ cup	**(*50 mL*) milk**
¼ tsp	**(*1 mL*) paprika**

■ In 1½-quart (*1,5 L*) saucepan over medium heat, in hot margarine, cook onion until tender. Stir in soup, sour cream, milk and paprika. Heat through, stirring often.

■ Serve over vegetables, beef or rice.

To microwave: Reduce margarine to 1 teaspoon (*5 mL*). In 1½-quart (*1,5 L*) microwave-safe casserole, combine margarine and onion. Cover with lid; microwave on HIGH 3 minutes or until onion is tender, stirring halfway through cooking. Stir in soup, sour cream, milk and paprika. Cover; microwave on HIGH 3 minutes or until hot, stirring halfway through cooking. Serve as directed above.

Makes about 2 cups (500 mL).

CORN CHOWDER

1 tbsp	**(*15 mL*) margarine *or* butter**
½ cup	**(*125 mL*) chopped onion**
½ cup	**(*125 mL*) chopped green pepper**
½ tsp	**(*2 mL*) dried dill weed, crushed**
1 can	**CAMPBELL'S condensed Cream of Potato Soup ***
1 can	**CAMPBELL'S condensed Cream of Celery Soup**
2 cups	**(*500 mL*) milk**
½ cup	**(*125 mL*) water**
1½ cups	**(*375 mL*) frozen whole kernel corn (sweet corn)**
⅛ tsp	**(*0,5 mL*) black pepper**

■ In 3-quart (*3 L*) saucepan over medium heat, in hot margarine, cook onion, pepper and dill until vegetables are tender.

■ Add soups, milk, water, corn and black pepper. Heat to boiling, stirring occasionally. Reduce heat to low. Cook 5 minutes. Garnish with *fresh dill*, if desired.

** If not available at your food market, substitute 1 can CAMPBELL'S condensed Cream of Celery Soup and add 1 medium potato, cooked, peeled and diced (⅔ cup / 150 mL).*

Makes about 6 cups (1,5 L) or 6 side-dish servings.

SHRIMP CREOLE SOUP

1 can	**CAMPBELL'S condensed Tomato Soup**
1 soup can	**water**
½	**green pepper, chopped**
½	**small onion, chopped**
½ cup	**(*125 mL*) cooked rice**
½ cup	**(*125 mL*) coarsely chopped cooked shrimp**
¼ tsp	**(*1 mL*) Louisiana-style hot sauce**
	Fresh dill sprigs for garnish

In 1½-quart (*1,5 L*) saucepan, combine soup and water. Add pepper, onion, rice, shrimp and hot sauce. Over medium heat, heat through, stirring occasionally. Garnish with dill, if desired.

Fish Creole Soup: Prepare Shrimp Creole Soup as directed above, *except* substitute *1 fish fillet*, cooked and flaked (½ cup / *125 mL*), for the shrimp.

Makes about 3½ cups (875 mL) or 3 side-dish servings.

SHORTCUT EGGS BENEDICT

1 can	**CAMPBELL'S condensed Cream of Chicken Soup**
⅓ cup	**(*75 mL*) milk**
1 tbsp	**(*15 mL*) lemon juice (optional)**
6	**slices (1 oz / *30 g each*) Canadian bacon *or* 12 strips bacon, cooked and drained**
3	**English muffins, split and toasted *or* 6 slices bread, toasted**
6	**poached eggs**
1 tbsp	**(*15 mL*) finely chopped parsley**

■ In 2-quart (*2 L*) saucepan, combine soup, milk and lemon juice. Over low heat, heat through, stirring occasionally.

■ Meanwhile, place 1 slice of bacon on each English muffin half; top each with 1 egg.

■ Pour ¼ cup (*50 mL*) of sauce over each egg and sprinkle with parsley. Serve immediately.

To microwave: In 1-quart (*1 L*) microwave-safe casserole, combine soup, milk and lemon juice. Cover with lid; microwave on HIGH 4 minutes or until hot, stirring halfway through cooking. Continue as directed above.

Makes 6 main-dish servings.

SHORTCUT EGGS BENEDICT

CHICKEN-BROCCOLI DIVAN

1 lb	**(*450 g*) fresh broccoli, cut into 2-inch (*5 cm*) flowerets, cooked and drained**
1½ cups	**(*375 mL*) cubed cooked chicken *or* turkey**
1 can	**CAMPBELL'S condensed Cream of Broccoli *or* Cream of Chicken Soup**
⅓ cup	**(*75 mL*) milk**
2 tbsp	**(*30 mL*) dry bread crumbs**
1 tbsp	**(*15 mL*) margarine *or* butter, melted**

■ Preheat oven to 450 °F (*230 °C*). In 10- by 6-inch (*25 x 15 cm*) baking dish or 1½-quart (*1,5 L*) casserole, arrange broccoli and chicken. In mixing bowl, combine soup and milk. Pour over broccoli and chicken.

■ In bowl, combine bread crumbs and margarine; sprinkle over top. Bake 15 minutes or until hot.

To microwave: In 10- by 6-inch (*25 x 15 cm*) microwave-safe baking dish, arrange broccoli and chicken. In small bowl, combine soup and milk. Pour over broccoli and chicken. In bowl, combine bread crumbs and margarine; sprinkle over top. Cover with waxed paper; microwave on HIGH 6 minutes or until hot, rotating dish halfway through heating.

TIP: You can substitute 1 pound (*450 g*) fresh broccoli, cut into spears *or* 1 package (10 ounces / *285 g*) frozen broccoli spears, cooked and drained, for the broccoli flowerets.

TIP: If you like, sprinkle ½ cup (*125 mL*) shredded *Cheddar cheese* or 2 tablespoons (*30 mL*) grated *Parmesan cheese* over soup mixture *before* topping with the crumb mixture.

Makes 4 main-dish servings.

1 Place broccoli and chicken in casserole.

CHICKEN-BROCCOLI DIVAN

2 In mixing bowl, combine soup and milk.

3 Pour mixture over broccoli and chicken.

4 Sprinkle breadcrumb and margarine mixture over top.

CLASSIC MACARONI AND CHEESE

1 can	**CAMPBELL'S condensed Cream of Celery Soup**
¾ cup	**(*175 mL*) milk**
1 tsp	**(*5 mL*) prepared mustard *or* mild English mustard**
⅛ tsp	**(*0,5 mL*) pepper**
3 cups	**(*750 mL*) cooked elbow macaroni (1 cup / *250 mL* uncooked)**
2 cups	**(*500 mL*) shredded Cheddar cheese (8 oz / *225 g*), divided**
1 cup	**(*250 mL*) French fried onions, optional**

■ In 1½-quart (*1,5 L*) casserole, stir together soup, milk, mustard and pepper. Stir in macaroni and *1½ cups* (*375 mL*) of cheese. Bake at 400 °F (*200 °C*) for 25 minutes or until hot. Stir.

■ Sprinkle with remaining ½ cup (*125 mL*) cheese. Top with onions, if desired. Bake 5 minutes more or until cheese melts.

Makes 6 side-dish servings.

CHILI CON CARNE

1 lb	***(450 g)*** **ground beef**
½ cup	***(125 mL)*** **chopped onion**
2 tbsp	***(30 mL)*** **chili powder**
1	**clove garlic, sliced *or* minced**
1 can (15 oz)	***(425 mL)*** **kidney beans, undrained**
1 can	**CAMPBELL'S condensed Tomato Soup**
¼ cup	***(50 mL)*** **water**
2 tsp	***(10 mL)*** **vinegar**
	Hot cooked rice, optional

■ In 10-inch *(25 cm)* skillet over medium heat, cook beef, onion, chili powder and garlic until onion is tender and beef is thoroughly cooked and no pink remains, stirring to separate meat. Spoon off fat.

■ Stir in beans, soup, water and vinegar. Heat to boiling. Reduce heat to low. Cook 10 minutes, stirring occasionally.

■ Serve over rice, if desired.

To microwave: Into 2-quart *(2 L)* microwave-safe casserole, crumble beef. Stir in onion, chili powder and garlic. Cover with lid; microwave on HIGH 5 minutes or until meat is no longer pink, stirring halfway through cooking to separate meat. Spoon off fat. Stir in beans, soup, water and vinegar. Cover; microwave on HIGH 5 minutes or until bubbling, stirring halfway through cooking.

Makes 5 main-dish servings.

CLASSIC TOMATO SOUP-SPICE CAKE

2 cups	**(*500 mL*) all-purpose flour**
1⅓ cups	**(*325 mL*) sugar**
4 tsp	**(*20 mL*) baking powder**
1½ tsp	**(*7 mL*) ground allspice**
1 tsp	**(*5 mL*) baking soda**
1 tsp	**(*5 mL*) ground cinnamon**
½ tsp	**(*2 mL*) ground cloves**
1 can	**CAMPBELL'S condensed Tomato Soup**
½ cup	**(*125 mL*) shortening**
2	**eggs**
¼ cup	**(*50 mL*) water**
	Cream cheese frosting, optional
	Fresh strawberries *and* mint for garnish, optional

■ Preheat oven to 350 °F (*180 °C*). Grease and flour two 8-inch (*20 cm*) round cake pans.

■ In large bowl, combine flour, sugar, baking powder, allspice, soda, cinnamon, cloves, soup, shortening, eggs and water. With mixer at low speed, beat until well mixed, constantly scraping bowl with rubber spatula. At high speed, beat 4 minutes, occasionally scraping bowl. Pour batter into prepared pans.

■ Bake 35 to 40 minutes or until wooden toothpick inserted in center comes out clean. Cool in pans on wire racks 10 minutes. Carefully remove from pans; cool completely. Frost with cream cheese frosting, if desired. Garnish with strawberries and mint, if desired.

Makes 12 servings.

CLASSIC TOMATO SOUP-SPICE CAKE

SHORTCUT VICHYSSOISE

1 can	**CAMPBELL'S condensed Cream of Potato Soup ***
1 soup can	**milk**
1 tsp	**(*5 mL*) snipped fresh chives *or* parsley**

** Not available in the U.K.*

■ In 1½-quart (*1,5 L*) saucepan over medium heat, stir together soup and milk. Heat thoroughly, stirring occasionally. Stir in chives.

■ Pour mixture into blender container. Cover; blend until smooth. Refrigerate at least 4 hours.

■ Thin to desired consistency with additional milk. Serve in chilled bowls. Garnish with additional *chives*, if desired.

Makes about 2½ cups (625 mL) or 3 side-dish servings.

QUICK GAZPACHO

1 can	**CAMPBELL'S condensed Tomato Soup**
1 soup can	**water**
1	**small cucumber, peeled, seeded and chopped**
1	**stalk celery, chopped**
1	**small carrot, chopped**
2	**green onions (spring onions), sliced**
1 tbsp	**(*15 mL*) lemon juice**
	Celery leaves for garnish

■ In large bowl, stir soup. Gradually stir in water until smooth.

■ Add cucumber, celery, carrot, onions and lemon juice. Cover and refrigerate at least 2 hours before serving. Garnish with celery leaves, if desired.

Makes about 3 cups (750 mL) or 3 side-dish servings.

HAM-AND-CHEESE CHICKEN ROLLS

4	**skinless, boneless chicken breast halves (about 1 lb / *450 g*)**
4	**thin slices (½ oz / *15 g each*) cooked ham**
4	**thin slices (½ oz / *15 g each*) Swiss *or* Emmental cheese**
2 tbsp	**(*30 mL*) vegetable oil**
1 can	**CAMPBELL'S condensed Cream of Broccoli *or* Cream of Chicken Soup**
⅓ cup	**(*75 mL*) milk**
¼ cup	**(*50 mL*) sliced green onions (spring onions)**
⅛ tsp	**(*0,5 mL*) dried thyme leaves, crushed**
	Fresh parsley for garnish

■ Flatten chicken to even thickness using palm of hand or flat side of meat mallet. Place 1 ham slice and 1 cheese slice on *each* breast half. Roll up chicken from narrow end, jelly-roll fashion. Tuck in ham and cheese, if necessary; secure with wooden toothpicks.

■ In 10-inch (*25 cm*) skillet over medium-high heat, in hot oil, cook chicken rolls 10 minutes or until browned on all sides. Spoon off fat.

■ Stir in soup, milk, onions and thyme. Heat to boiling. Reduce heat to low. Cover; cook 10 minutes or until chicken is no longer pink, stirring occasionally.

■ To serve, spoon some sauce over chicken rolls; pass remaining sauce. Garnish with parsley, if desired.

Ham-and-Cheese Turkey Rolls: Prepare Ham-and-Cheese Chicken Rolls as directed above, *except* substitute 4 *raw turkey cutlets* (about 1 pound / *450 g*) for the chicken. *Reduce* cooking time for browning the turkey rolls to 5 minutes.

Makes 4 main-dish servings.

1 Flatten chicken breasts with a meat mallet.

2 Place ham slice and cheese slice on chicken breast.

3 Roll up chicken from narrow end.

HAM-AND-CHEESE CHICKEN ROLLS

4 Cook chicken rolls 10 minutes, browning on all sides.

5 Spoon off fat.

6 Stir in soup, milk, onions and thyme.

Follow these guidelines for storing perishable foods in the refrigerator or in the freezer.

- Raw meat and poultry should be wrapped securely so they do not leak and contaminate other foods or surfaces. Use plastic bags *over* commercial packaging.
- Since repeated handling can introduce bacteria to meat and poultry, it's best to leave the product in the store wrap unless the wrap is torn.
- Date any undated products you may have purchased and be sure to use them within the recommended time.
- Eggs should be stored in their carton in the refrigerator not in the door since repeated opening and closing of the door elevates temperatures.
- Make sure the arrangement of items in your refrigerator and freezer allows the cold air to circulate freely.
- To minimize dehydration — "freezer burn" — and quality loss, use freezer wrap, freezer-quality plastic bags or aluminum foil *over* commercial wrap on meat and poultry that will be stored in the freezer for more than two months.

These short but safe storage time limits will help keep refrigerated food from spoiling. The time limits given for frozen foods are to maintain maximum flavor and texture. It is still safe to eat frozen foods that have been kept longer.

Product	Refrigerator (40°F) (*4°C*)	Freezer (0°F) (*-18°C*)
Eggs		
Fresh, in shell	3 weeks	Don't freeze
Raw yolks, whites	2-4 days	1 year
Hard-cooked	1 week	Don't freeze well
TV Dinners, Frozen Casseroles		
Keep frozen until ready to serve		3-4 months
Deli & Vacuum-Packed Products		
Store-prepared (or homemade) egg, chicken, tuna, ham & macaroni salads	3-5 days	Don't freeze well
Store-cooked convenience meals	1-2 days	Freeze these as soon as you get home, not *after* they've sat in the refrigerator
Soups & Stews		
Vegetable or meat-added	3-4 days	2-3 months

Product	Refrigerator (40°F) (*4°C*)	Freezer (0°F) (*-18°C*)
Hamburger, Ground & Stew Meats		
Hamburger & stew meats	1-2 days	3-4 months
Ground turkey, veal, pork, lamb & mixtures of them	1-2 days	3-4 months
Lunch Meats		
Meats, opened	3-5 days	In freezer wrap,
unoponed	2 weeks**	1-2 months
Bacon & Sausage		
Bacon	7 days	1 month
Sausage, raw, from beef, pork or turkey	1-2 days	1-2 months
Smoked breakfast links, patties	7 days	1-2 months
Hard sausage, pepperoni, jerky sticks	2-3 weeks	1-2 months
Ham, Corned Beef		
Ham, canned, label says "keep refrigerated"	6-9 months	Don't freeze
Ham, fully cooked, slices	3-4 days	1-2 months
Fresh Meat		
Beef steaks	3-5 days	6-12 months
Beef roasts	3-5 days	6-12 months
Lamb chops	3-5 days	6-9 months
Lamb roasts	3-5 days	6-9 months
Pork chops	3-5 days	4-6 months
Pork roasts	3-5 days	4-6 months
Veal roasts	3-5 days	4-8 months
Meat Leftovers		
Cooked meat and meat dishes	3-4 days	2-3 months
Gravy and meat broth	1-2 days	2-3 months
Fresh Poultry		
Chicken or turkey, whole	1-2 days	1 year
Chicken or turkey, pieces	1-2 days	9 months
Cooked Poultry, Leftover		
Cooked poultry dishes	3-4 days	4-6 months
Pieces, plain	3-4 days	4 months
Pieces covered with broth, gravy	1-2 days	6 months

**Source: U.S. Department of Agriculture-Food Safety and Inspection Service.*

***But no more than one week after the "sell by" date.*